WILDERNESS

TRIAL by WILDERNESS

David Mathieson

Houghton Mifflin Company
Boston

Library of Congress Cataloging in Publication Data

Mathieson, David, 1941–
  Trial by wilderness.

  Summary: A girl survives a plane crash off the
coast of British Columbia, and then faces survival in
the wilderness, a feat which calls upon her courage,
her endurance, and her skills.
  [1. Survival—Fiction] I. Title.
PZ7.M4265Tr 1985   [Fic]   84-27766
ISBN 0-395-37697-1

Printed in the United States of America

HC ISBN 0-395-37697-1
PB ISBN 0-395-56456-5

AGM 10 9 8 7 6 5 4 3 2

Prologue

Like a clock running backward, the altimeter unwound. The rate of descent gave them a little over two minutes, before they hit the sea.

Beside him, Elena worked her way into the flotation jacket one arm at a time, hampered by the seat belt. She was taking it well, he thought. At such a time, the temptation would be to fight the hand through the sleeve, using too much force. But this young passenger of his was being most methodical about it. In the silence of the power-off glide he could hear the zipper being pulled up.

"Just as a precaution," he said. "Try to make yourself go limp when the time comes. And *breathe out*. Empty your lungs, OK?"

Calm, intelligent eyes. The sunlight made the area behind the dark glasses visible, but darkened the blue of the irises to a deep teal color. The lips said yes, she understood. The head bobbed and the sun ran in the short, pale hair in a blaze of gold.

"No sweat," he continued. "This airplane floats like a duck. Your dad's got a transceiver at camp, doesn't he?" Another nod. "That's good. He'll know who to contact. They'll have a plane over us before . . . before we have a chance to get at the sandwiches. So don't worry. The odds are with us."

He lied.

They'd be flying blind soon.

He was taking them to a stretch of the Canadian coast where, at best, they would find only reefs and sea stacks. It was either that or hit a mountain.

Ahead, the sun abruptly turned orange and feeble. A moment later it went out. They flew inside a canyon of gray vapor, and the floor of the canyon rose up to swallow them. It was like going from June to November. The air in the cockpit grew chill, and small worms of moisture crawled on the other side of the Plexiglas, driven by the slipstream.

Silently, he cursed himself for a fool.

Old man Tate had warned him. "Gotta watch it, son. Off the islands this time of year you'll get a real pretty day. See clear to Alaska! And that's when a fog'll nab you. Five, six o'clock. Hours till sunset yet, but it'll start building up. Real fast. So what you do is you watch the bays. The shady side of a mountain maybe. Comes quick, and when you spot it, don't waste no time. Get the crate down and wait it out. Nothin' else you can do."

Only . . . what if you've got a radio you can't get to transmit? What if you're head-down, fussing with the blasted thing, and don't catch on in time? And then, when you try VHF, you can't get it to *receive*.

No Omni.

What do you do then, old man?

You put her down willy-nilly, that's what you do. You take a perfectly healthy airplane and play *tag* with it. In the fog. With the rocks. And a fellow named Elmer Tate loses one of his airplanes. *That's* what!

And a pleasant, elderly archaeologist, Bradbury by name, opens the flap of his tent and looks off down the inlet, wondering if that soft gray stuff up there means his daughter'll be a little late.

Yes, Doctor Bradbury. Elena is going to be a little late getting out to the dig this year.

The girl with the quiet, introspective manner; the girl who almost never speaks; the one who, nevertheless, still manages that sudden, heart-warming smile . . . is going to be a little late.

"Look!" she said.

The thing she wanted him to see rushed at them obliquely. *Go to the right*, he thought. *Firewall it.*

The trees of the mountain were darker now, blurring by the left wing — around and under as the plane began its bank. There was a hissing sound below: branches, rushing against the floats, punctuated by a machine-gun rattling. And then they were clear . . . slipping to the right. He leveled the wings, aware of an increasing vibration. Like a truck on a washboarded road.

Must have got the prop, he thought. Have to shut her down. She'll tear the engine out of the mounts if I don't.

They were still in a dive. He chopped power, brought the nose up. The prop was windmilling, but at least the vibration had been eased.

For the first time he was able to take a hopeful breath. The fog here was less dense. He could see water below. Green and smooth. Putting down on it would be a piece of cake.

Except for the rock.

It would do, however. Like a ramp. Tear up the floats a bit, but otherwise good enough.

Down now. It sounded like a ton of gravel roaring down a chute. He knew what it must be doing to the floats.

Still, it didn't cut their speed.

He had time to put the control wheel forward, to tramp left rudder as they went off the end.

He had time to hear the silence. Like that of a glider. And he spoke to the plane, as if it were a person.

"Come on, old girl. Don't *yaw* like that. You'll hit the wrong —"

And then the time was gone.

1

Elly didn't feel it at first. She only saw it.

Water flowed quietly around her shoes. On the surface drifted small bits of . . . the stuff looked like cork. Other than that, the water was clear. Like water in a mountain stream.

Except it wasn't cold.

Calmly, logically, she deduced that it *ought* to be cold. And only after reaching this conclusion did she actually feel how cold it was. She also became aware of the control yoke pressing against her ribs, and the constriction of the seat belt.

She was facing sideways, with her left shoulder against the control panel. The way she was turned, she could look out the side window and watch the plane's wingtip slowly, slowly descend until it touched the water — where it stopped.

The water around her legs kept rising.

Small creaking, groaning noises came from the structure of the aircraft, but other than this it was quiet.

She pushed herself upright, and the movement triggered a small avalanche to the left. The cabin was a wreck. The cargo in back had moved forward into the place where the pilot had been sitting. It was a wall of canvas-covered parcels, surveyor's equipment, luggage — all entangled with the tie-down straps that should have held it in place.

The water had reached her hips now. She wasn't sure what to do.

"Jim?" Her voice sounded metallic, machinelike inside the enclosure. "Jim! Are you all right?"

She couldn't see anything of him. He was hidden behind the cargo. A sudden, horrifying insight came to her: if she couldn't get him out, he would drown.

It shocked her into action. Desperately, she worked to push away the wreckage. Lighter pieces she threw in back. The bigger ones wouldn't budge — they were held by a net of cords and straps, knotted together. She knew about knots, and worked quickly. The first came undone. She went on to the next, praying for time.

But the plane went down with a rush. She barely had a chance to lift her face, to suck in one last breath before going under. Everything became green and blurred. Over the sound of escaping air, she heard a measured thudding. She listened to this — the beating of her heart — while struggling with the door. She decided the door was jammed and wouldn't open.

It did more than open. It detached completely, vanishing into the darkness below.

With new hope, she started to rise from the seat . . . and

was unable to move. A dozen heartbeats went by, pounding ever louder in her ears, but struggle though she might, she was still a captive.

Finally, she remembered the seat belt.

Undoing the clasp, she swam from the cockpit, turned face up, and pulled herself to the front of the wing. The light called from above. But for the second time she was held back. The plane, she realized, was traveling forward as it sank. There would be no escaping past the leading edge of the wing, for she couldn't fight the current.

She let go. The light went away. In the dark, she could feel the wing sliding by her face. When it was gone, she allowed the gentle, friendly hand of the flotation jacket to take her up, and came at last to the air.

For companions, she had a metal pontoon and a floating yellow pencil. Off in the mist, barely visible at a distance of a hundred meters or so, was the rock.

The best solution to the problem, she thought, would be to climb aboard the pontoon and paddle it like a surfboard until she reached the rock. The pontoon, however, proved traitorous. It floated bottom-up, and when she tried to pull herself onto it, the structure rolled toward her, like a log, and she slipped. A saw-toothed edge of aluminum ripped open the palm of her left hand. The pontoon then sank, leaving her alone in the water with a bleeding hand.

Several minutes had already gone by. A person could expect to survive the waters of the Northwest for a quarter-hour or so. She thought she'd have more time than this herself, as the jacket was lined with plastic foam, a good insulation. She wasn't suffering from the cold as yet. Nevertheless, it would be foolish to waste time. There might be a current, bearing her away from the rock.

She began with a crawl stroke.

To her astonishment, she found she simply wasn't moving. At the end of a minute, the pencil was no farther away.

It was the jacket! Its flotation layer made the thing stiff and bulky. It was like a parachute below the water. The sleeves, when she lifted them to take a stroke, were like enormous, water-filled sausages.

The jacket couldn't be left behind, however. Once she got to the rock (*if* she got to the rock) she'd die of hypothermia in a matter of hours without the insulation it afforded.

And yet it was beginning to look as if she'd die anyway, before reaching the rock, *because* of the jacket. A classic double bind!

Grimly, she began experimenting. She tried every face-down stroke she knew. None was any better than the first.

She rolled face up, trying a backstroke. Now she made a small amount of progress. The pencil began to recede. Not rapidly, but at least it *was* receding.

The labor of swimming became uncomfortable, then painful, then agonizing. It was like an endless race. A sprint followed by another sprint. Doggedly, she kept at it, for she knew her life was in the balance. She had to ignore the pain of breathing, and the incredible, burning cold at the back of her neck. She swam on, her mind strangely clear despite the pain. She thought of her father, and of the sailboat he had found for her; it would be at the dock, waiting for her. She thought of the house in Victoria. And in the end she found she didn't care about any of it. The only thing that mattered was to stay alive — this would be such a *foolish* way to die. The search planes would come in the morning, and they'd find nothing but a dummy, a stupid puppet floating lifeless in a big orange jacket. It would be a disgrace. And so she went on.

Another few meters and she wouldn't have made it. She lost all sense of direction, all sense of up or down, and fought blindly in her pain, and it was this that brought her feet into contact with the rock. She was able to stand and to walk beyond the water.

The enormous labor of swimming with the jacket had produced a carry-over effect. For a time she felt remarkably warm again, and the pain in her chest went away. Her cut hand had begun to hurt, but at least it no longer bled. She congratulated herself on being alive and reasonably alert. Her chances, as she saw them, were good. Thanks to the jacket, she could last until morning. Then the fog would clear and the planes would come.

She began a survey of her island. It was a flat slab of stone, tilted up at one end. Along its length, the rock was marked with fresh gouges — the track of the pontoons. Here and there lay chips and slivers of aluminum, while right at the crest, not far from where a small driftwood log was balanced, she found a curious metal cap, pressed tightly around a knob of rock. The scrap of metal from the plane had struck the knob so forcefully that the texture of the rock underneath could be seen through the aluminum. It had welded itself in place.

By now, the effect of the exercise had worn off and she was feeling chilled. More chilling still came the realization that the tide was on the rise.

"So *that's* why the log is at the top of the rock," she said to herself. "Because the tide left it there."

Suddenly she felt like weeping, and closed her eyes. For a while she stood, with the tiny droplets of fog brushing softly against her face. They made minute pinpricks of coldness as they traveled on the breeze.

She must resign herself to yet another effort, she decided. It was the only way. If she stayed where she was, she'd drown during the night.

Somewhere, there was a mountain. They'd almost run into it with the plane. She'd be safe there; she'd be able to rest. And, just possibly, the mountain was but a short distance away.

"And possibly it *isn't!*" jeered the voice of Defeat. "Just *possibly* you'll head in the wrong direction!"

Ignoring this, she rolled the log to the water. She found a balk of driftwood and broke it in half. The halves went alongside the log: one to port, one to starboard. They'd act as sponsons, for stability. It made a feeble excuse for a raft, but no other timber was available. She removed her wool shirt and used it as a rope to tie the three timbers together at the bow. Then she sat astride the log at the stern, the roots against her back, and clamped the after ends of the sponsons to the log with her knees.

Even with her legs submerged, the raft barely floated. It was also extremely unstable. One false move would cause her to tumble sideways into the water. The raft would then disintegrate, and in a few minutes she would be dead.

It took every scrap of her will power to leave the rock behind. Paddling with her hands held inside the sleeves of the jacket, she headed to windward, steering by the slight riffle on the water. Not by accident had she chosen this course. The long scratches in the rock astern had pointed the way to the concealed mountain — the direction from which the plane had come.

Upwind. In the silence and the fog.

After a time she began to shake with cold, and the shaking threatened to overturn her. To make matters worse, the breeze died. She was in the lee of the mountain: near enough for the wind to be blanketed, but not so near as to make the mountain visible.

"It will happen to you, just as it happened to Jim," said Defeat.

"Not yet," she replied.

She shouted into the fog with all her might. Again and again. At first there was no reply, but after laboriously turning the cranky little raft to face in the opposite direction, she began hearing a faint echo.

Evidently she had traveled half a circle since losing the wind.

Methodically, she hunted for the source of the echo. It led her on a frantic yet slow-motion chase through the fog, a little to one side, then a little to the other.

She began to understand now. There were two echoes.

But gradually the two became louder. The interval

between shout and reply shortened. A heaviness appeared in the fog. Under it ran a pale band. And under that, a strip that was quite dark.

A steep, dark beach. Made of stones.

Pale driftwood above.

And forest. A wall of forest.

2

"Their last report put them here, two hundred kilometers south of us."

She could see the gesture her father would use, pointing with the stem of the pipe she'd given him at Christmas. He and Alex would be in the radio tent, with a chart spread before them.

"There's a chance they're alive. An excellent chance, don't you think? Engine trouble. That's what this Tate fellow thought, and he ought to know. They'd simply land in the water. The strait's calm. They'll be in fine shape. At least . . . they should be."

Alex, the practical one, is drawing a pencil line on the chart. The line runs northwest from the plane's last position, parallel with the coast. Somewhere along it is the spot where the plane is to be found.

Alex, perhaps, is less hopeful than her father. He is a flyer himself, and would have a better idea of what the fog the evening before might mean. He would also be thinking about the loss of radio contact. He'd keep it to himself, however. Alex would be more likely to draw attention to the number of planes available for the search. He would be looking up the time of sunrise, saying: "The light'll be strong enough for them to take to the air before long. Some of the planes'll be in the search area by breakfast."

For the tenth time since the crash she pushed the stud on her watch . . . to be reminded once again of what the salt had done. Instead of the warm glow of lighted numerals, she saw only the reflection of a gray dawn. The watch was dead.

Her shivering had eased enough by now for her to undo the clasp. Taking off the watch, she peered at the back of the case. It was still too dark for her to decipher the engraved words, but that didn't matter; she knew them by heart.

> *For my cherished Elena*
> *on her 16th birthday*
> *Father*

She cried for a time, thinking of that birthday of a year and a half before. Then she slipped the watch back in place, and began swinging her arms and stamping her feet in the gravel of the beach.

The night had been more hideous than anything she could have imagined. She had spent it huddled at the base of a tree. Part of the time her knees had been tucked under the jacket for warmth. Other times, she'd been forced to stand to regain circulation. Her face still ached from clenching her teeth against the cold, and sleep had been impossible. Even with her eyes open, the darkness had flamed with images. A waking nightmare endlessly repeated itself. Again and again the pontoon had reared above her, like a ship lifting its stern as it sank. The rudder would sidle downward, threatening to snag the jacket and drag her under, and when it was gone there was the blood from her hand, staining the water.

But that was now past. Such things could not survive the light of day; already she was feeling more herself. She began walking along the beach, keeping the water on her right. The exercise warmed her. After a time, she came to a place where the angle of the beach increased and the rounded stones clattered and yielded underfoot. In the gloom, it was hard to stay upright, so she turned and headed back.

The water was to her left now, and noticeably brighter than before, reflecting the light of the sky without trace of a ripple. Not even the long, slow movement of a swell.

Interesting.

It meant she was on the protected inner shore of a bay, or at the very least, a channel.

Abruptly, the beach came to an end, blocked by a great monolith. The evening before she had been unable to see the top of it clearly, due to the fog. Now the thing looked like a medieval fortress, rising vertically from the beach, the outer portion reaching into the water, the landward side linked to the mountain by a series of turrets and ledges. The resemblance to a castle didn't stop here. The beach around her was peopled with dark shapes. Over the centuries, blocks of stone had split away from the solid ramparts above, and now stood watch below the wall. Like the men of an army, assembled at a spear's length from one another.

As night became day, the stones took on a less forbidding aspect. The great monolith itself seemed less like a fortress. It was, after all, only a tall stone pinnacle. Out in the water stood part of the same formation — the summit of another spire — this one hidden in the water and only showing its top as the tide receded.

She was shocked to realize that this was the very rock on which she had landed the night before. It looked so remarkably innocent, like the smooth, rounded back of a whale. One had to look closely to see the glint of aluminum on it.

Beyond, the mist had begun to lift from the water. She saw that her deduction had been correct: she was on the shore of a bay. It was a long bay, with a narrow opening to the sea, a channel framed by tall headlands. The surrounding mountains were immense, rising straight from the water. It seemed incredible that trees could grow on a slope that steep, but grow they did. The somber embrace of the conifers was unbroken.

She was inside a well, a forested well.

Fortunately, though, the well had been created on such a titanic scale that an aircraft could maneuver within it.

"They'll be low enough to catch sight of someone on the beach," she said to herself, "especially if that someone is waving an orange jacket."

There was something else she could do to attract attention. But it would be best for her to move away from the pinnacle first, so the view from the air would not be obstructed.

Going to the place where the beach was steepest, she dragged pieces of weathered timber down from the level of the driftwood, arranging them against the dark stones to form the letter H. She made the H fifteen paces high by nine paces wide, and it was nearly an hour before the thing was complete. Clearly, the task would be a formidable one, for each of the three remaining letters would have to be in proportion to the first.

She wiped the sweat from her eyes, took off the jacket, and went on working. She had to use great caution, extracting her building material from the timbers at the top of the beach. The enormous logs along the outer edge were easily dislodged, and she remembered well the lesson of the night before, when the first log she touched had gone crunching down the incline and into the water like a quick-moving steam roller.

And so the work progressed. The H was followed by an E, which was followed by an L, which in turn was followed by the letter P.

She debated whether or not to add an exclamation mark, but decided enough effort had been invested. Low tide had arrived, which meant it was about six in the morning. From now on she would try to avoid noisy activities, such as dragging timbers over stone, and to keep an ear tilted toward the sky.

Perched comfortably in a natural seat of driftwood, she watched a flight of puffins skittering above the water. Puffins were such comical birds — with their great triangular beaks and drooping ear tufts below, they seemed to be dragging long pieces of seaweed about with them.

With surprise she realized that her various discomforts, both physical and emotional, had all but disappeared. She was watching the flight of birds with genuine pleasure. Despite the loss of sleep, she didn't feel tired. Her hand wasn't hurting much. Her clothing was nearly dry.

And she was becoming hungry.

Naturally! It was breakfast time.

She bestirred herself and went to look for berries at the edge of the forest. This proved to be unexpectedly difficult. The only level surface in this place was the top of the bay itself; everything else tended toward the vertical. The side of the mountain had been worn away at the tide line to create a slight notch. This was what held the driftwood. Above rose a small cliff of marl, three or four meters high. The branches of the cedars and spruces rested against the lip of the bluff, and peeping out underneath were the smaller plants: briars and an occasional huckleberry bush. Since it would have been dangerous to search the edge of the bluff from above, she had to do so from below, balancing on the driftwood, scrambling up the network of roots to reach the level of the deciduous plants.

All in vain. There were no blackcaps among the briars. The sprays of Oregon grape and huckleberry held only fruit that was green and inedible.

Slowly working her way along the bluff, she came once more to the stone barrier of the pinnacle. Here the ground was moist, and the long canes of the salmonberry grew in profusion. She was overjoyed to see clusters of light-colored berries underneath the leaves. When she climbed within reach of them, however, she found only the deceptive white cores where the berries had been. Birds had beaten her to the harvest. Just a single berry remained: an amber jewel, full of fluid, but with little flavor.

She had no sooner swallowed the berry when she felt a powerful thirst. The cool, tantalizing liquid was a reminder of the dryness of her mouth and throat. It had been over half a day since she'd had anything to drink — a cup of coffee before the plane took off — and here she'd been working hard all morning, exhaling moisture. Sweating.

She thought of how cool and silvery everything had looked a few hours earlier. Now the layer of morning dew was nearly gone. As the day had grown warmer, the fresh water covering the beach had evaporated. Even the greenery along the bank held only an occasional droplet. She had failed to use a source of drinking water while it was available.

Feeling a tremor of alarm, she climbed into the darkness of the forest. It took a moment for her eyes to adjust, but then she was relieved to find that her guess had been correct. Evaporation had not been as rapid in the shelter of the trees. The broad sprays of sword fern were still beaded with dew. She wouldn't be denied water after all.

There remained the problem of collecting it. Most of the water escaped when she tried to use her hands, for she needed to keep the cut in her palm dry. Then she hit on the idea of skipping the intermediate step. Instead of collecting a small pool of water in the palm of one hand and then trying to drink it, she used her tongue to collect the water.

She felt foolish at first, lapping at the ferns as if she were a cat. It worked, though, and one couldn't argue with success.

Little by little, she drank, bending above each plant, being careful not to disturb the fronds and spill their delicate cargo. She stopped every so often to listen for the sound of an engine, but the forest and the waters of the bay were silent.

She lost track of the number of ferns. A few drops from each frond, a small sip from each plant. It was a tranquil, hypnotic activity. And it had a quality of stealth about it. She felt as if she were in another era of the earth's history: the time of the early mammals, when small, warm-blooded creatures had to live secretly, out of sight of the great lizards.

"At least that's one thing I *don't* have to worry about," she said to herself. And then she gave a start. A pair of eyes were less than a meter away.

If the frog hadn't blinked she would never have noticed him, for his green markings were such excellent camouflage on top of the moss. He was a large, healthy-looking frog, and she was puzzled that he should be so indifferent to her presence. Then she saw that two of his legs, front and back, were pinned together at a strange angle. Above the apex formed by the two limbs glared a second set of eyes. The unwinking, slitted eyes of a snake.

Neither the frog nor the snake made any response as she slowly knelt down to watch. It appeared to be a stalemate, each party to the contest patiently waiting for the other to make a move.

She didn't interfere. Although her sympathies were all with the frog, she didn't think the snake could do much damage. Snakes had to swallow their food whole. In this case, a medium-sized snake had caught himself an extremely large frog. Sooner or later he'd have to admit that this particular meal was simply too big to eat. Especially sideways.

She went about her business and left them to theirs. Later, when she was no longer thirsty, she stopped by to see how the duel was progressing. Neither had moved.

She returned to the beach and found that a breeze had sprung up. Small waves broke against the stones. The tide, she noticed, was only halfway in.

Nine o'clock or so, maybe ten. And still no sign of the troops.

Her eye followed the uneven sequence of gravel beach and marl bluff as it meandered off to the left. After a kilometer or two it ended in a small promontory. This restricted her view of the rest of the bay, and she wondered what lay beyond.

All along, her assumption had been that the bay was uninhabited. But she couldn't be certain there were no people until she'd seen all of the shoreline. "I'd look awfully silly," she told herself, "having to be rescued within walking distance of a marina . . . or near a scientific outpost like my father's."

For the first time in many hours, she laughed. Tossing the orange jacket on her shoulder, she set off along the tide line, whistling as she went. A few of the notes came echoing back to her, sounding as if someone were dogging her footsteps. The echo soon faded, however, as the pinnacle fell away behind.

3

It sounded like the purring of a cat. An ordinary sound, easily ignored: heard, and yet *not* heard.

A detour through the forest had become necessary, for there was no beach at this point, only the sheer marl bluff. She walked along a fallen log in the green darkness, aware of an occasional glint of water far below.

Halfway along the log, she began to notice the purring noise. Realization came like an electric shock. She whirled and ran back the way she'd come. Clearly, there wasn't time to reach the shore. She stopped at the base of a large tree, an arbutus, the kind some called a madrona. It stood at the top of the bluff, half uprooted and leaning out beyond the surface of the forest. Leaping onto one of the great, level branches, she scuttled along on hands and knees to reach the open. The branch dipped and swayed as she neared the outer end. But she was clear of the forest now. The dying tree had dropped most of its leaves. She was high in the open air and the jacket was in her hand, ready for waving.

She tried to control her breathing: tried to listen. But nothing could be heard.

No. There it was again! She could hear it growling away in the distance. Off beyond the pinnacle — beyond the headlands at the entrance to the bay.

It was out over the sea. A large aircraft, she could tell. There were several engines. She could hear the way they throbbed, rumbling along at low altitude. A big old flying boat — that's what it sounded like.

The sound traveled from north to south along the shore of the island. Then it faded in the distance.

She hadn't caught so much as a glimpse of the plane. Now it was gone.

She had only the mountains and the bay, the beach and the pinnacle. The wind could be heard, moving softly in the trees. Small waves lapped the base of the bluff.

She felt afraid, looking down. Distance made the rocks below look small and sharp. Before, she hadn't noticed, so intent was she on signaling to the plane. To go back she had to turn around, and as she did so, the branch began to shake as if it wanted to throw her off. She completed the journey in a rush. At the place where the limb grew large and solid again she collapsed in relief and lay still, resting her face against the satiny bark.

One thing was certain: they had not been searching for her. It was just a transport flight — people and freight — trucking on down from Alaska. They'd been too far out, flying too low to be looking for a downed plane.

For the second time that morning she wept, her tears darkening the smooth reddish bark of the arbutus.

Continuing her journey, she reached the promontory, only to be faced with another disappointment. What had appeared to be a clearly defined point of land, the portal to another arm of the bay, was actually only a slight bulge in the line of the shore. The beach ahead was a replica of the one behind, uniting smoothly with a section that had been visible to her from the start.

No sign of people. No trace of either a stream or a spring in all that long and desolate shore.

With a heavy heart, she returned to the pinnacle. The day had grown warm despite the overcast. Her pulse prodded like a dull knife at each temple, and she was thirsty again. Even the driftwood signal distressed her. It was like the work of an aborigine, wanting to talk with gods in the sky.

Remembering her encounter of the morning, she climbed the now familiar stretch of bluff into the forest and found again the little battlefield in the moss. The snake had shifted his position and held both the frog's rear feet in his mouth, having released the forelimb. Other than this, the situation was unchanged.

"Just be patient, little friend," she said to the frog. "He'll give up before long. You're too big for him. When he lets go and you've become your own frog again, I'll make a nest for you out of moss; you can ride in the pocket of my shirt. Tell you what: I'll take you home with me when the plane comes. I'll fix up a box with ferns and a pool of water, and I'll find things for you to eat."

Stimulated by the sound of her voice, the frog flexed his arms. The slender, human-looking hands clutched at the moss. Behind, the snake made a quick biting motion to get a better grip. She felt like forcing the snake to let go, but decided it would injure the frog more than if the snake disengaged on his own.

In spite of herself she had to smile, thinking what her friend Pauline would say about these two:

"Calories, chum! *Calories!* Doesn't matter where they come from — not if the old pack's empty. Got to keep your strength up, remember! Alive or not, it's still food."

Pauline the mountain climber. If one could choose a companion for such an occasion as this, that companion would have to be Pauline. Laughing, ebullient Pauline: dark hair tied back in a fluffy pony tail; her every gesture, every word, intuitively quick. "Hell! Just kick open a rotten log and eat the grubs inside," she'd said one time. "It's what keeps the *bears* fat, it'll feed you too!"

Elly could only shake her head at the memory. If there was a survival food Pauline was *not* prepared to eat, it had yet to be mentioned.

Just thinking about Pauline was enough to raise her spirits. She, Elly, might be ignorant of the fine points of filleting raw snake meat, but such a thing would probably not be required. Her own expertise lay with the sea. And that's where she was — along a salt-water beach.

"So you see, little friend, you have nothing to fear," she said. "Even if it takes them days to find me, there won't be any reason for me to turn traitor and eat a pet frog. There are other things available."

She stroked the top of the small head and received a lethargic blink in answer.

"As for *you*, Mister Snake, you're just lucky my name isn't Pauline!"

She rose and went to try her luck at barnacle hunting along the base of the pinnacle. Reaching into the water with a stick, she smashed apart a colony of acorn barnacles that clung to the rock just under the surface. Fishing out the slippery lumps of tissue with her fingers, she collected a mound of the stuff, placing this on a weathered board, which served as a platter. It was not appetizing. Except for the fishy smell, it was like ground-up snail meat. She forced herself to swallow part of it, but had to lay the rest aside. The little that she ate left a foul, salty taste in her mouth.

It had been a mistake. What she needed most was water, not food.

The sun came out and filled the beach with glare. As if summoned by an evil magic, swarms of beach fleas appeared. Clouds of them leapt from the gravel at her every step. They hissed against the cuffs of her jeans; she could feel them crawling on her ankles. Continually, she had to stop and shake them off. A high, singing noise filled her ears. For a time she thought this might be the sound of a plane, but it came from within, not from without. She retreated once more to the forest, feeling lightheaded and miserable. She wanted to see her frog again, but when she reached the place the only thing left of him was a single green hand, reaching from a corner of the snake's mouth. The snake's forebody looked like a fat sausage, stuffed almost to bursting. The jaw had literally detached itself from its moorings to accommodate the body of the frog.

She wanted to kill the snake, but knew it would do no good. The frog was past saving. The constriction of the snake's gullet would have brought suffocation by now. The convulsions that now shook the encased form were only a reflex . . . to the acids of the snake's digestive tract.

The tiny hand gave a final twitch and slipped from view. The snake, its lipless mouth closed at last, writhed heavily away into the forest.

"I'm sorry, frog," she whispered. "I was wrong."

She felt suddenly ill, and vomited the pieces of barnacle meat. The kaleidoscope was being shaken. Images flashed and tumbled, and then resolved themselves into a picture that no longer moved.

Her future self. Lying on the beach beneath a crawling blanket of fleas.

Eyes unable to blink; mouth unable to close.

She saw it with such clarity that her only thought was of escape. The beach — and the hideous thing that lay there — had to be left behind.

And so she began to climb.

4

It was a place of sunlight and wind.

Light so intense it made the eye want to stop seeing; wind so strong it was difficult to remain standing.

The way led upward at times, but more often the spine of the monolith ran level, as if she were tramping the backbone of an armored dragon whose head lifted far beyond the forest and out over the waters of the bay.

In places the rock crumbled underfoot. Small fragments would run away to either side, hop once or twice, then plummet out of sight.

The wind grew stronger as she went, but was less of a threat after she reached the broad top of the outer spire. This formed a small country in itself. There was a field of dry grass, a thistle plant with a purple blossom, and at the very end, a contorted little spruce, looking like a tree in an oriental print.

One of the branches made a handhold for her, which left her other hand free to shield her eyes. To the south and west, the direction of the afternoon sun, the water coruscated like a living, fragmented mirror. It made her long for the dark glasses she'd worn during the flight.

Gone now. No chance of ever getting them back. They'd be down in that drowned and ruined cockpit, not far from the man who only yesterday had rummaged in a flight bag to find them . . . out of concern for her eyes.

Unexpectedly, the thought of the pilot aroused a feeling of remorse. Guilt!

But that was foolish; she'd done her best to get him out — her absolute best.

Even so, she had to turn away, for the sight of that empty stretch of water east of the whale-shaped rock disturbed her.

Looking off to the west, she began piecing together what had happened. And she decided they'd been lucky. At least in the beginning. Instead of hitting the cliffs to seaward, they had managed to thread a needle in the fog. All unknowing. Once inside the bay, the plane had approached the ridge to the north obliquely. It had given them warning — a chance to turn eastward. And the shape of the bay had been favorable, too. Shaped like a boomerang, the bay curved as if to accommodate their change of course. The entire eastern reach had lain ready for a landing.

But the luck had run out, over against the side of the mountain. She could see the freshly scarred wood, even at this distance. Some of the branches hung like corpses on a gibbet, weathered and silvery. Overall, the snag had the shape of a skeletal hand, reaching out from the forest.

In contrast to the dead tree, the smooth, whalelike rock

out in the water seemed harmless and peaceful. At this stage of the tide, two smaller rocks had risen nearby, like a pair of whale calves swimming in the company of the mother.

Innocent. Yet deadly.

She thought again of the pilot . . . and then something large and gleaming rose up beside her. She cried out, partly in surprise and partly in pain, as her shoulder came in contact with the sharp stub of a branch.

Ruefully, she laughed. What was more to be expected near the sea than a gull?

The bird had come sweeping up the face of the cliff, borne on the wind. An enormous fellow, pure white underneath. The outspread fan of the tail tilted from side to side as the gull balanced in the updraft. He looked back at her once, under his wing, before sliding away out of sight.

Even though he'd given her a start, she felt all the more lonely, seeing him leave.

The wind rushed and buffeted, tossing her hair awry, whipping her shirt collar against her throat. In surprise, she discovered that her tongue and the inside of her mouth had become as dry and smooth as porcelain. Henceforth, she decided, she would have to keep her lips tightly shut against the wind. At another time, this curious sensation of smoothness might have been interesting. Now it caused her to wander the top of the rock in agitation.

Coming to a raised place, she found a small bronze plate, grouted into a hollow in the stone. Under a heavy coating of grime was a little cross with a punch mark in the center, and the inscription

$$B. B. — c pt 8$$
$$alt. 209.1$$

Not much instruction there, other than the fact that her thigh and the palm of one hand were currently resting at an altitude of two hundred and nine feet above sea level.

Feet, not meters: the old system of measurement.

Fifty, sixty, possibly eighty years before, men with theodolites and colored flags had come. They'd stayed for a time, completed their survey, placed a marker, and then they'd left. Long, long ago.

But she could see the way they must have looked, with their wool shirts, black suspenders, hobnailed boots. They would have carried old-style canteens; large and round and chugging with water.

She realized the thing had gone too far when she not only saw it, but could *hear* it as well. A man in a wool shirt and engineer boots had lifted a canteen to his lips. And she heard the flutter of water as he drank.

Nor could it be made to go away.

She kept *hearing* something!

It came and went with the wind. A mechanical . . . *flapping* noise.

She stood up.

It sounded exactly like someone shuffling a pack of playing cards, slowly and deliberately.

The sound grew louder when she went toward the

west. And it became louder still back toward the land-ward end of the pinnacle. It sounded now like the beating of a pair of wings, and she had a sudden vision of the beautiful sea bird, trapped in a crevice, trying desperately to free himself.

Her heart went out to him. Hesitating only a moment, she slid down the canted brow of the pinnacle, straining to see more of what lay below. The farther she went, the steeper the slope. She depended on friction alone now. There were no crevices in which to hook her fingers. But the closer she came to the rounded edge, the louder the noise became. She was worried about the gull — and afraid of sliding. Once begun, a slide would be impossible to arrest, and so she brushed away every particle of sand and grit before trusting her weight, thinking all the while of the way she had slipped on the surface of the pontoon. This, however, was not metal. It wasn't slick with water the way the aluminum had been. It was grainy to the touch, and she would know when she was pushing the limit.

Her progress toward the curving threshold of the cliff revealed more of the underlying beach. It was sandy and smooth, like a sheet of concrete. And just coming into view was a tiny figure. Dappled gray and white.

The gull. Strutting, bird fashion, along the sand. Obviously without a care in the world.

Her concern had been for nothing.

The sound came without interruption now, loud enough to be heard over the heaviest of the gusts, when the wind thrummed against the face of the cliff. The source of the noise was just out of sight, somewhere within the

strip of beach directly below, inside the territory ob-
scured by the last meter of rock.

There was no question of going any farther, however.
The limit had been reached.

Down below, the gull left a meandering trail of footprints. He came to a brighter patch of sand and stopped,
surveying his domain, the yellow beak pointing this way
and that. He was paying no attention to the fluttering
noise.

And she noticed something else.

The patch of lighter sand, actually a raised place in
the beach, was only light when contrasted with what was
nearby. Elsewhere, the sand was just as bright and dry
as the mound under the bird's feet.

With infinite caution, she withdrew to safety, crawling
up the angled face of the rock, all the while telling herself
not to hurry. "Nothing's going to change over the next
few minutes," she told herself, "so don't do anything
foolish."

After the smooth, treacherous lip of the western cliff,
the journey back along the spine of the pinnacle seemed
relatively free of risk. She was tempted to run in places,
but controlled the impulse. The trip down through the
forest went by in a blur. Suddenly she was at the edge
of a marl bluff. Beneath a curtain of low-hanging branches
she could see the strange beach. In contrast to the one
on the other side, this beach was nearly level, the smooth
sand stretching for a considerable distance before it met
the water.

She couldn't lower herself to the driftwood from here,

she decided; it was too much of a drop. She'd have to go along the bluff to the west.

When she did find a way down, it was at a spot where the beach reverted to shingle. She stumbled and fell among the rounded stones, but picked herself up. Upon reaching the sand, she broke into a run.

No sign of the gull. Evidently he'd flown away.

To the right, the beach curved in a great crescent toward the end of the pinnacle. To the left stood a mountain of driftwood, piled at the base of the cliff. Somewhere between the bay and the driftwood would be the place where the bird had been standing. As she approached, she spotted the familiar line of webbed footprints. Over where the gull had begun his walk, the prints were not as well defined, being only a set of scratches in the beach. There was a reason for this. Here the sand was more solid; it changed from a light tan color to dark brown, due to the presence of moisture. The surface was quite firm, not soft and yielding as was the drier portion of the beach.

She stopped.

She had hoped that a stream might lie inside this dark area of sand. But there was no stream. She stood looking at the place where the stream should have been, fighting a wave of frustration.

Softly, from her left, there came the sound that earlier had drawn her to the brow of the cliff. There was no apparent explanation for it. The wooden mountain was tall and formidable, the weathered tree trunks lying higgledy-piggledy, as if cast aside by a capricious giant. Such was the confusion of the scene that it took a moment for a small detail to register.

From under the driftwood ran a thin bright ribbon. It branched upon the sand, dividing into small fingers that spread and sank from sight.

Again she ran. She knelt beside the small channel and pushed the knuckles of her uninjured hand into the beach, letting her palm fill with water.

It was fresh, and very cold.

5

Exhaustion struck with as little warning as an avalanche. One moment she was kneeling beside the stream, drying a hand on her jeans, and the next she was fighting to stay upright. It was as if the weight of her body had been multiplied several times.

In reaction against it, she got to her feet. Not since childhood had she experienced this particular sensation. She'd forgotten what an agony the need for sleep could be, how the mind began to misbehave.

"Brain!" she said firmly. "You will *not* stop functioning! You *cannot* go to sleep!"

This seemed to produce an effect. As a test, she calculated the length of time she'd been awake:

Up at six. Traveling most of the day. Aboard the plane by midafternoon . . . crashed around dinner time.

Twelve hours to that point.

Signal completed by six the next morning, making an additional twelve hours.

Twelve added to twelve was twenty-four.

Right. It was now midafternoon. To the total of —
what was it again? Twenty-four! — should be added . . .

She had to use her fingers. It was a long time before
she had the answer: somewhere in excess of thirty-two
hours. Thirty-four maybe.

That was *one* thing accomplished at least.

She tried to remember what the other was — the other
thing she had to do.

Ah!

The sound reminded her. It was like a team of horses,
clopping along a paved street over on the other side of
the driftwood.

Climbing was easier than thinking; it could be done
automatically. Standing atop the wooden mountain, she
found herself at the entrance to a small cove, hollowed
out of the marl. It was a triangular space: marl bluff on
one side, the stone wall of the pinnacle on the other.
The clopping sound came from a narrow grotto at the
back, at the junction of marl and stone.

She slid down the inner face of the driftwood and
started across the floor of the cove. Immediately, her feet
began sinking in mud. Enormous leaves grew out of the
marsh, each one reaching as high as her waist. It was
like a science-fiction movie. The great, plastic-looking
leaves smelled like a skunk.

Hastily, she returned to the security of the driftwood.

She discovered a wide ledge at the base of the pinnacle. Seeing that it led in the right direction, she followed it. The moss covering the ledge was a brilliant
green, and ran with water every time she took a step.

At the entrance to the grotto there was a shallow pool. A train of ripples swept its surface. When she looked around the corner she saw, on a level with her eyes, a hanging scrap of moss suspended above the pool. Large dollops of water formed and broke, a steady succession of them. It happened with machinelike regularity.

A dripping faucet, minus the plumbing.

It wasn't even very loud . . . not up close. But she could see how the sound was channeled and sent upward. The grotto acted as a speaking tube, directed toward the edge of the cliff above.

She turned and sloshed back along the ledge. The way led into a tunnel. She walked along the tunnel, running into things in the gloom, for one wall was made of driftwood. The tunnel came to an end, opening out above the beach, while the ledge continued on toward the end of the pinnacle.

She stood looking down at the sand below.

To fall, or not to fall, that was the question.

She leaned forward, but changed her mind at the last minute and jumped to the top of a boulder. The rock was shaped like a divan, raised at one end, hollowed in the middle.

It would do very nicely, she thought, spreading the jacket on the rock. The sun felt comfortably warm after the chill of the grotto.

She was about to lie down when a flash of motion caught her eye, over at the edge of the bluff. Instantly, she leapt from the rock and ran across the sand.

"Hey! Leave those alone!" she shouted. She threw a

stone. Finding a piece of wood, she threw that. "Those are *my* berries!" she called after the last of the retreating birds. "Go find your own!"

This was, of course, absurd, as the birds had already found their berries and were now being unjustly deprived of them.

"I'll cry about it later!" she declared fiercely, reaching for a cluster of ripe red huckleberries.

They made anything but a full meal for her, but walking the beach afterward, she felt deliciously lethargic. Her feet dragged. Every time she scuffed a shoe against the sand, a loud squeak emerged. The same note each time. Without fail.

She scuffed up and down the beach, puzzling over this — listening, drawing pleasure from the sound. She could still hear the *squeak-squeak-squeak* of it when she opened her eyes. It echoed in her memory even as she realized that she was lying on top of the rock. She was frightened for a moment, trying to recall what had happened, and then she remembered climbing once more onto the rock and folding the jacket to make a pillow.

She had slept for hours. The beach was now in shadow, and the mountains across the bay glowed in the mellow light of sunset.

Feeling cold, she put on the jacket and curled up again, cushioning her head on her arm. Listening to the tapping of the water inside the grotto, she closed her eyes. The wind could be heard, up among the turrets of the pinnacle, and there was the far-off cry of a bird of prey: an eagle.

Imperceptibly, the sound wove itself into the fabric of a dream.

She accompanied the eagle as he flew. They soared together until the air became turbulent and dangerous for them, whereupon they flew to a high rock. Now the eagle was no longer an eagle. He was a man. The pilot.

It's familiar. This great pinnacle of stone, the forested mountains, the wind, the square of metal set in the rock.

The little bronze marker is between them, and in front rests a wicker basket. A picnic basket.

Overcome with the beauty of her surroundings, she turns to her companion and smiles happily.

There is an answering smile in the pilot's eyes. They have no need for speech.

Resting a hand on the bronze marker, he tells her, without words, how the charts he used aboard the aircraft came to be made. It is all founded on the location of this one lump of metal.

She understands completely.

But still something worries her. Something she wants to ask. She looks the question across to Jim and traces the plane's course within the bay: through the entrance, along the mountain, into the tree and down.

Why? she asks. Why so soon?

In answer, he holds up a little wooden trap. It has been sprung. The soft, plump body of a mouse dangles from one end. The head of the mouse rests on the wood, the small nose pressed against the bait.

Yes, she tells him. I know — mousetrapped. But *why?* What was the reason for cutting the engine so soon?

She shows him Whale Rock, and how they could have flown above it and landed safely in the water beyond. There was no need to crash!

Why, she wants to know, *why* stop the engine?

He looks at her. Then he uses his voice for the first time. "The c.g.," he says simply.

She feels a surge of irritation, for it doesn't answer the question. She demands to be told. What is this c.g.? What does c.g. have to do with shutting down an engine? The plane couldn't clear the rock because the engine was dead!

Jim's hand is on her arm. He raises a finger.

Watch. Listen.

Using the gestures of an aviator, he demonstrates how the plane flew. He shows the engine and how heavy it is. How strong it is. When an engine fights to get loose, no mounting bolts will hold it. She should know that.

See? query the hands.

The engine breaks loose and falls away.

And now she does see. It *does* have to do with c.g., for with the heavy engine no longer in place, the center of gravity moves back toward the tail. The delicate balance is destroyed. The plane's weight isn't centered under the wing where it belongs. Tail-heavy, the aircraft points its nose straight up.

They would have fallen out of the sky. Backwards.

She realizes now why he had to kill the engine when he did. There was no other choice.

I'm sorry, she tells him, reinforcing the message with her hands. I'm not angry anymore. I simply didn't understand the reason. So please don't go away. If I said the wrong thing, could you forgive me? Could you stay with me?

But he is changing already.

She watches his expression freeze and his eyes look to the distance, and she feels a despair she has never known before. She plunges on, wanting to show him how rare and valuable a thing it is for them to be able to understand each other. They are able to do this because . . . because they both can read a chart. They use charts of different kinds, but the principle is the same. Air chart, nautical chart; it makes no difference. Both are based on the same logic, on the same piece of bronze resting in the rock.

You see? You see? she tells him, using words herself now. There's no reason for you to leave.

The wind has grown into a hurricane. The wicker basket is carried away. Pieces of debris hurtle past. She is thrust against him by the wind. Terrified of being blown over the edge, she throws her arms around him. But the shape beneath the flyer's jacket is rigid and unyielding.

The man's neck is as cold as stone against her cheek.

6

The days remained clear and warm; not a trace of dew could be found in the mornings. Without the trickle of water from the marsh, she would never have survived the third day.

During this time there were no planes — at least, none that offered hope. Following the passage of that propeller-driven craft of the first morning, the sky was empty, save for the high-flying jets, drawing their thin trails against the stratosphere. She might as well have been on another planet as far as they were concerned. Only a radio signal could have reached them.

The moon also traveled the sky. It was nearly full, and thus worked in concert with the sun to produce enormous tides. At daybreak, the water reached almost to the marsh. Then, in a few hours, the level would drop five meters. By midmorning, a great expanse of sand would lie uncovered, reaching toward the end of the pinnacle. In these latter stages of the run-out, a mass of large, plum-colored barnacles crowded the foot of the cliff, hissing and clicking inside their shells.

She left them strictly alone, remembering how ill she'd been after eating their smaller cousins, the acorn barnacles. Something better was available in any case. Hidden beneath the surface of the beach at low tide lay a wealth of butter clams. She had only to dig a shallow trench to find all she could eat. A few minutes of effort produced dozens of the fat little shells, cream-colored and marked with an attractive pattern of ridges.

Lacking fire for cooking, she had to eat them as soon as they were dug. Nor could she use subtlety in reaching the meat. The swift, downward blow of a rock was the only way. Once the fragments of the upper shell were removed, the semiliquid interior had to be swallowed whole, like a raw egg.

She longed for cooked food, and so spent much of the second day working with dry pieces of wood, rubbing them together in various combinations to create point sources of heat. Evening came, but still not a wisp of smoke had been raised. Either her material was too damp, or else there was something to the technique she didn't understand. Taking a rusty nail from a driftwood timber, she tried striking it against stone. A forlorn hope, and she knew it. One needed flint as well as steel to obtain a proper spark, and, as far as she knew, the Northwest had no deposits of flint. As expected, the experiment with the nail was no more successful than the first approach.

She ate the last of the ripe berries the next morning.

That left only the raw clams and a few dandelion leaves as a source of food. Hoping to find another patch of ripened berries, she made an expedition to the west, searching every likely spot along the way. Beyond the area of sand, the country was identical to that seen on the first morning, on the other side of the pinnacle. Steep shingle; a long bluff of yellow clay; a train of mighty logs, resting precariously at the top of the beach. After several kilometers, the beach became nothing but a jumble of boulders. Beyond, even these disappeared and there was only the water, lying deep and green beneath a rocky cliff. It would have cost her hours of slogging to reach the seaward face of the island through the forest, so she turned back.

There had been no berries ripe enough to eat.

Nonetheless, the trip hadn't been a total waste. Being nearer the sea, this western beach offered a better variety of salvage. She found a ten-centimeter length of barbed wire, three rusty staples, eight nails, and a plastic bottle that had once held liquid bleach.

She put the bottle to immediate use upon her return to the pinnacle. Now she could transport sea water and create a pool atop the divan-shaped rock, where there was a deep indentation. The pool made a good storage place for clams, keeping them safely alive until needed. In this way, mealtime was no longer dependent on the tide. At high water, when the clam beds were submerged, she still had access to her catch.

She was developing a keen eye for what might prove useful — and an even keener memory. She now recalled a shattered glass jug on the other side of the pinnacle.

Since the route up the mountain and around was so tedious, she tried going around the outer end, down near the water. To her surprise, this was not only possible, but fairly easy. One followed the ledge from the point where it left the tunnel, did a bit of toe and finger work to traverse the outer face of the monolith, turned the corner, and behold! Right at the point where it became impossible to travel farther along the cliff, there stood one of the stone soldiers, at attention in the water, just a couple of meters away. All she had to do was bring out a long pole, vault from the face of the pinnacle to the top of the first soldier, and from there to the next, and so on, until she gained the beach. It took skill, this pole vault from stone to stone, and the first time she tried it she nearly ended in the water. But by the time she had made several trips — carrying shards of glass both large and small in her pockets — the knack of using the pole had become second nature.

Only later did she think of the implications.

She bedded down for the night among the ferns up in the forest. Tired though she was, she couldn't sleep. She was haunted by the memory of four smiling faces in a photograph: father, mother, daughter, son. They'd been in the news for a time, that family. Their light plane had crashed in the mountains, in the snow. Killing the son. Leaving only three.

The father had gone for help, despite his injuries, and was never seen again. So that left only two.

The mother and daughter shifted the frozen body of the young man into the back seat and huddled together in the front. Trying to keep warm. To pass the time they kept a diary and fashioned a pack of playing cards from slips of paper. Toward the middle of December, the words "Guess Daddy didn't make it," were written in the diary. A few weeks later came the entry "What's the matter Search and Rescue? Can't you get your act together? Hope you had a real *good* Christmas."

A couple of healthy, uninjured women. Playing cards. Waiting for rescue.

They might have built a shelter, made a fire, heated tea, and kept themselves warm in the process. But they didn't. They had gasoline, tools, a supply of metal and cloth and leather. They could have made a smoke signal. They could have made snowshoes. Or skis. They could have explored their surroundings.

But they didn't.

They waited. And played cards. Growing ever more feeble as the weeks passed.

Unlike many such planes, gone astray among the mountains, this one was eventually found, for it was close to a highway — just on the other side of a ridge. Inside the fuselage they found three mummies: two female, one male. And they found the diary. And the little pack of homemade cards.

Elly shuddered, and the ferns crackled under her.

Hadn't she been guilty of the same reasoning?

Take that first afternoon on the other beach. She had accepted the notion that *both* sides of the pinnacle would be dry. There had been no reason for her to think this. But it was what she had assumed. The discovery of the spring had been a fluke — and it *shouldn't* have been. She ought to have postulated the existence of the spring and gone looking for it. She should have set out to test the theory, instead of following this vague assumption of hers.

It was an appalling error.

Except for happenstance, she would by now have paid the ultimate penalty for that little slip in logic. And the way around the barrier was so incredibly simple! As quick and easy as picking up a pole and hopping a few stones. Yet it had taken her three days to think of it, days when she'd been adequately supplied with water. And food. Suppose there *hadn't* been any water during that time. How inventive would she have been? How agile of mind, with a body screaming with dehydration? How much thought would she have given then — to the game that might be played with a pole?

She knew the answer to that, and it made her shudder anew. "From now on, Bradbury," she commanded, "you are going to pay more attention to *what if* . . . and *how might*."

She fell asleep thinking of a light plane, of a snowy glade in the mountains, and of a highway, just on the other side of the ridge.

When she awoke, the sky was gray. A cold, hard wind blew from the southwest, kicking up a chop inside the bay. The waves roared against the beach, and when she went to retrieve her morning allotment of clams from the storage pool she felt the icy sting of the spray. Breakfast was a sorry affair. She drank a lot of water just to get it down, and this made her shiver all the more. When the time came for her to surrender the jacket, her courage nearly failed.

The first step had been to erect a stout post in the middle of the beach. After placing the jacket orange side out around the post, she took a branch and inserted it through the sleeves, scarecrow fashion. In the damp sand below she wrote:

NEED HELP
PLEASE WAIT
E. Bradbury

Turning her back on the crashing surf, she ascended into the forest. By comparison, it seemed very silent and dim, as if an eclipse were in progress. She had expected to see a squirrel or two, or at the very least a bird; but this near-vertical world of the deep forest was curiously barren. Nothing but fungi, colored white and brown, a few black millepedes, an occasional spider. The trees, she noticed, were not the familiar Douglas firs she had known at home. They looked like firs, but the foliage was different. The needles were more yellowish, and the bark was wrong. It made her feel misplaced, not to know what kind of trees they were.

For an hour she climbed, and still the slope continued upward to the limit of vision. The view when looking down was the same. She was beginning to develop a new respect for the size of this mountain. She had a vivid impression of why there were no roads in this part of British Columbia — and very few people. In all the hundreds of kilometers between Alert Bay and Prince Rupert there existed only a few tiny enclaves of civilization, a few scattered villages among the mountains and fiords. Travel between was by air and by water, never by land.

Abruptly, the crest of the ridge was upon her. There had been no gradual easing of the contour underfoot, no change in the foliage overhead. Simply an end to the climb and the appearance of a second abyss, identical to the one behind. The word "hogback" came to her, though in this case there was no jutting of rock, only the needle-blanketed crest leading away on either hand like the upturned blade of a wedge.

There was danger here. The only clue she had to her direction was the trend of the mountian. Now, with two slopes, she'd have to remember which was which. An absent-minded step, a turn of the head, and she'd lose track. In such vast wilderness, without supplies, map, compass, with nothing but the great roof of the forest overhead, one might wander forever. Or, more realistically, until one could wander no more.

Cautiously, she retreated down the southern slope a short distance and built a large tripod of dead branches. This, she told herself, would indicate the way back.

She returned to the crest and sat down with her back to a tree, facing the unknown, untraveled side of the mountain. Looking back over her shoulder, she could still see the tripod; turning to the front, she could be confident that she was facing north.

She sat quietly, listening. An hour passed. She didn't move except to place an elbow on each knee, cupping her hands behind her ears. Only the wind could be heard, sweeping the upper layers of the forest — that, and an occasional tapping, rattling noise as a needle or a twig tumbled down through the branches. Her mouth began to feel dry, so she drank some of the water in the plastic bottle, which she had carried up the mountain buttoned inside her shirt.

She capped the bottle and tucked it away. With her hand, she made a small clearing among the needles. Inside the clearing she built a palisade of twigs, equipping it with a gate. She made a blockhouse. And a flagpole. From a scrap of lichen she carefully fashioned a tiny flag and was in the act of fitting the flag to the pole when she heard a sound not caused by the wind.

So focused had she been upon the possibility of distant sound that it was a shock to hear something within the forest itself. Instead of the far-off note of a chainsaw, the chugging of a boat engine, the clink and pound of firewood being split — or any of the other noises she had hoped to hear — there now came a faint rustle, punctuated at intervals by the crunch of rotten branches under a heavy weight.

It was coming from below and to the right. After a time, she caught sight of movement. It was difficult to see clearly, with tree trunks in the way, but something tan-colored and large was moving up the slope toward her. The movement was almost languid: a rolling, pivoting, undulating flow against the side of the mountain. Even before the complete silhouette could be seen, she knew what it was.

7

The grizzly halted directly below, less than sixty meters off. She could see his vast head swing from one side to the other, and hear his breathing.

It was the bear's sense of smell that worried her.

Without warning, the doglike nose dipped out of sight, and just as quickly reappeared. A small branch cartwheeled off amid a shower of needles. Slowly, the animal began moving upward again, his course apparently chosen at random. He was only forty meters away when he veered to the left. She had just taken her first breath of relief, however, when the bear turned in her direction once more. She didn't think he'd caught her scent, but if he came much closer he would have to be nearsighted indeed to avoid seeing her.

Her chance came the next time he stopped. The bear's head was hidden; only the massive hindquarters could be seen.

She stood up and quietly slipped around to the other

side of the tree. Face pressed against the rough bark, she waited, listening. There was nothing but silence.

After a time the waiting made her edgy. She risked a look, but immediately pulled back. Had the bear been looking up-slope instead of at the ground he would surely have noticed a light-colored head against such a dark background.

What she needed was camouflage.

She looked at the sleeve of her shirt: a plaid in medium blue and gray. At a distance, the two colors ought to look innocuous. She was about to put the plan into action when a sudden bout of crunching noises erupted.

She came close to bolting.

Fortunately, she curbed the impulse. Despite the uproar, which sounded like sledgehammers striking a pile of cardboard boxes, the bear didn't appear to be coming any closer.

Her entire body had begun to vibrate, even those portions resting against the tree. Deciding that the motion was too slight to be visible at a distance, she slowly raised her right arm and extended the elbow past the edge of the tree. Praying that the bear would think of this as a mere bulge in the contour of the trunk, she put her eye to the triangular opening between arm and tree.

The bear attacked something on the ground, his forepaws lashing out with swiftness and power, the great hump of his shoulders jerking back and forth. Splinters of wood and other debris filled the air, falling in a cascade down the mountain. The animal seemed immune to fatigue. After several minutes of pummeling this unseen enemy on the floor of the forest, he turned without pause to an energetic digging. Gouts of earth sprayed forth as though propelled from the mouth of a cannon. She could hear a grunting, panting rumble.

Gradually the violence ebbed. The bear began a leisurely inspection of the wreckage, at times digging his claws into a shattered timber and tilting it up to examine the underside, looking for all the world like a man opening a trap door. She couldn't imagine what he was doing, and at the end of half an hour she actually caught herself yawning. The physical responses to fear that she'd noticed earlier had vanished; the bear seemed less of a threat, spending most of his time with his head down in the hole he had dug. The moment for a graceful exit had arrived.

She gauged the route that must be followed, concluding that a retreat to the other side of the crest would be possible — if she used care.

But it was not to be. In the time her attention was diverted, the bear had managed to climb from his excavation and work his way diagonally up the slope, completely outflanking her position. He had done this without making a sound, and was now standing motionless, not ten meters away, gazing at her.

It was unfair! All she wanted was to be left alone!

Without a thought for what she was doing, she found herself shouting *"Bugger off, you bastard!"*

He appeared to be astonished. Half a ton of bear lost his footing on the side of the mountain; he had to turn sideways to catch himself. Perhaps driven as much by gravity as by his own choice, he broke into a run straight down the mountain. In a matter of seconds the creature had disappeared, though Elly could still hear the distant crashing of his progress.

Then even the sound was gone.

Out of curiosity, she went down to where the animal had been digging. It looked as if a bulldozer had been at work: there were pieces of rotten log, heaps of plowed-up earth. The fragments of wood were riddled with passageways, and a number of soft-bodied insects wandered about. They looked like termites. Instead of being white, however, they were the color of copper. These then were the survivors. She remembered what Pauline had said about how bears kept fat.

The thing happened without warning. Overhead, one branch creaked against another. She looked up, casually. It was her last memory of that time. There came a feeling of unsteadiness, of alarm . . . and then she was in another part of the forest, far from the great excavation dug by the bear. Her forehead rested against a tree and she was terribly, painfully out of breath. She knew she'd been running — leaping and sliding at a terrific pace, mostly down.

She didn't know how far she'd run, or in what direction, and it came to her that she was lost.

It would have been comforting to believe that she had headed instinctively for her friendly bay, for the place where she had left the jacket. But she had no memory of making the decision. The sound of waves coming from below might well be the sound of another bay entirely.

Descending to the beach, she felt a rising dread, for nothing looked familiar. It was a strange beach. The opposite shore loomed gray and distant. To the left stood a large formation similar to the pinnacle — but it was not *the* pinnacle, and her vision went dim with tears.

It was then that she noticed the little spot of orange. Shimmer though it might, she could not doubt its existence. It was the jacket, standing watch at the water's edge.

She almost collapsed from surprise. It *was* the right beach! She had simply come upon it from an unexpected angle.

Her relief over this was even greater than that felt at her reprieve with the bear.

She spent the remainder of that strange afternoon at the top of the pinnacle, building another signal; the one on the beach had long since been destroyed by the tide. This new signal, she hoped, would be semipermanent: the word MAYDAY, fashioned of cedar branches, anchored against the wind with stones. The five block letters were arranged in the shape of a cross:

$$\begin{array}{c} \text{D} \\ \text{M A Y} \\ \text{Y} \end{array}$$

It was, she thought, a more official-looking request than the word "help." The letters were much smaller this time, for the material had to be brought a long way, but placed against the light-colored western brow, they stood out in vivid contrast with the rock. The letters ought to be visible for a considerable distance, perhaps as far as the entrance to the bay. She concentrated on making their edges straight and the corners well defined. "The better to catch the eye," she told herself.

Three letters had been completed when a light mist began to fall. She went on with her work. Without the wind, there was an eerie quiet.

And then the silence was broken by the sound of a human voice.

Aunt Agatha's voice.

"Elena!"

Just the one word, uttered in the manner of a summons.

The sound had come from the direction of the stunted spruce tree at the end of the pinnacle. But when she looked, there was only the swirling mist.

It happened again several hours later. The mist had turned to rain. She was on the beach, hauling driftwood planks to the foot of the bluff when the voice of her friend Pauline came to her. From out of the air.

The planks she had gathered stood against the bluff. The original plan had been to hoist them into the forest and build a lean-to at the spot where she'd slept the last few nights. But the planks seemed to make a better shelter just leaning against the bluff. No need for a frame to hold them up; and the face of the bluff provided an extra wall.

There was another reason for abandoning the earlier site: the knowledge that she was camped on the territory of a grizzly. The bear, she suspected, would now perceive her as an enemy; should they meet again, the outcome might be different. Here on the beach the chance of early warning would be greater, as would her options for escape.

She thought about this while standing in the rain. She had made a hat for herself from one of the large leaves of the marsh. It was like a crude umbrella, secured to her head with a thin strip of cedar bark, knotted under the chin. "I must look rather amusing in it," she admitted. The thing worked, however. If she stood quite still, the downpour didn't touch her.

This business of hearing one's name was most curious — hallucination no doubt, but amazingly real. Even to the form of the name. The voice of her aunt had pronounced all three syllables, as always.

How typical. Sour, authoritative Agatha. Never a kind word. It was almost a relief, despite the circumstances, to be free of her constant disapproval. To be out from under.

Do this, do that.

Posture, Elena. *Manners*.

As if she were a child!

But Pauline — that was something else. Pauline always called her Elly-chum. Just remembering the sound of it made her wish for company. Someone to talk to.

"There haven't been any planes, Pauline. It's been four days now, and the only one to come by was way the bloody *hell* out to sea."

Pauline, of course, had she been there, would have clucked her tongue and shaken her head in that slow, ironic way of hers. "My!" she'd say. "You *are* in a state, aren't you? But really! It isn't all that bad, is it? Oh, I know, things haven't worked out the way you'd like. So what?" Then there'd be the tilt of the head. *"Like I always say . . ."*

"Yes. I know." Pauline, like the French, had a saying for everything. *"Such is life in the Great Northwest.* But that's for small things, Pauline. This time it isn't like soaking your shoes in a creek and laughing it off."

"But your shoes *are* soaked, so what's the difference?"

"There's a big difference. There's sand in them for one thing. An Achilles tendon has a blister. There's a place where a branch went through my sock and into my ankle. These low-cut shoes aren't made for hiking, you know."

"Hm-m-m," Pauline would say. "You've got a point there. But you haven't finished with the list, have you?"

"No. As a matter of fact, I haven't."

"Got a whole kit-bag of complaints, eh? Figure I haven't heard of this sort of thing. Like splinters, and bruises, and a bunch of little cuts and scrapes. Hands all banged up. Leg muscles all sore, just because you weren't in shape for that climb this morning. The old city-girl blues . . . But wait a minute!" A squinch-eyed, canny expression appears. "How about diarrhea? Bet those raw clams are really doing the job on you! How about it? Fess up, now!"

"Pauline . . . I don't know what I'm going to do. You know the routine better than I. Tell me. What am I supposed to do?"

"Well, for one thing, you can stop worrying about what you're *supposed* to do. It can't be done by the numbers. You have to improvise. If it's any consolation, you've taken a big step already — shifting the focus from what hurts to what might be done about it. That's something. Personally, I think it's time you started thinking of your own comfort. What you need — the thing you *really* need — is a fire. You want my advice? Here it is. First thing tomorrow, start a fire."

"But I've tried!"

"Oh, *that*. You give up too easily, kid. Really you do. There are more than a couple of ways to make a fire, you know. So give it a whirl. Think of the benefits. A little spruce-tip tea will clear up that digestive problem of yours in a wink. You'll be warm when the wind blows, dry when it rains. There'll be a world of things to eat. The heat of a fire will break down the starches in some of the plants you've got around here so your body can use them. The clams can be smoked. You could trap a few dungeness crabs and cook 'em, just like home. Heavens! you'll eat like royalty! There's just no end to the things you can do, once you've got a fire."

The rain pattered on the umbrella-leaf hat, and some of it seeped along the strap, dampening her neck. "I do need a fire," she said.

But now, the imaginary Pauline could only be made to smile and nod.

"You're a good friend, Pauline. I even know you well enough to guess what you'd say. If you were here."

Without a sound, Pauline's lips moved. Before her,

seated on the ground, were the members of her rock-climbing class — the way Elly had seen them the summer before. Upturned faces, young and old. Listening to Pauline.

In silence.

Elly wiped at the trickle of water on her neck. "Well. I'm a member of the Hermits' Club now! *Talking* to myself."

But it *had* been a good idea. About the fire.

8

Two small depressions in the surface of a dry plank: one of them circular, the second somewhat larger and shaped like a teardrop. The two shapes were linked, the point of the teardrop joining with the circle.

The idea was to rotate the end of a stick inside the smaller depression, generating heat, which would cause the shavings at the point of the teardrop to smolder. The living spark would then eat its way down to the main store of shavings, eventually causing the tinder to burst into flame.

This was her third attempt at making fire. Maybe the third time would be the lucky one.

It proved quite difficult, however, for her to rotate the drill. The palm of her left hand was far from healed; she had to use the inner surface of her left forearm instead. With the stick held between her forearm and the palm of the opposite hand, the action was extremely awkward. She developed a painful cramp. Although heat had been produced, there was no sign of scorching. No smoke.

So much for experiment number three, she thought. Time to try number four.

With a piece of salvaged glass, she carved a hole in one side of a wooden block. The upper end of the drill stick fitted into the hole and was lubricated with moist clam flesh to make it turn more easily. She could hold the block with the fingers of her left hand without pain, thus supporting the drill stick vertically and leaving her right hand free for rotating the drill.

It didn't work. The act of pressing down on the block increased the amount of friction. The flat of her right hand simply skidded past the side of the stick without turning it. She could still turn the stick with her fingers, but this was too feeble an action. To get hot enough, the hole in the fire board needed a lot of friction. It would take the power of her entire arm, not just her fingers. The back and forth motion of her arm had to be converted into a rotation of the stick.

There was the Stone Age method, of course. It was known as the bow drill.

But to make a bow, she needed a bowstring, a cord. And the cord would have to be extremely flexible, for it would take a complete turn about the drill. The loop thus formed would be traveling — quite rapidly and under tension — back and forth along the length of the cord as the bow moved.

Pieces of root, strips of bark, twisted fibers of grass — none of these would work.

But human hair might.

Using a thin sliver of glass as a knife, she chopped away, fairly close to the scalp, until she had a number of orderly bundles of hair. They would not be missed: she had taken a little here, a little there. The fibers were short — no longer than a finger — but they ought to serve well enough.

It took half the morning and part of the afternoon. Her fingers ached from holding the strands in tension while each was being spun. But at last the thing was done — a slender, three-stranded cord, less than a meter in length. It was bumpy and uneven, but she took pride in it. Selecting a sturdy branch, she tied the cord to the ends of it to make a bow. After moistening the hole in the upper block (to ensure that the clam flesh functioned as a lubricant and not as a glue) she looped the bowstring around the drill stick and tried again.

And still it didn't work! The surface of the new cord was smooth; it slipped on the drill like a piece of greased nylon. Obviously, the tension of the cord would have to be increased.

Bending the bow into a tighter curve, she retied one of the knots. Now, when she plucked the bowstring, it hummed.

She took a slow breath, trying to quell the butterflies in her stomach. "That first try didn't count," she told herself. "This is still experiment number five."

She saw to the tinder, brought the pile of kindling within reach, again moistened the bearing in the block of wood, twisted the drill stick into position on the cord, and fitted the end of the drill into its depression.

She put her knee on the fire board, held the bearing block with her left hand, keeping the stick vertical. Holding the bow in her right hand, she pushed it forward.

This time the drill turned. Rapidly.

She brought the bow back and there was no slipping. The cord reeled along as on a spool. She increased the tempo, and could hear the drill rubbing inside the hole. The cord made a whirring, bicycle noise. There was no smoke as yet. She was afraid of stopping, even though curiosity made her want to take the drill out and see if the end was getting warm — that would only waste heat. And something might go wrong. There might not be another chance.

Still no smoke. There was a smell, though. The tang of scorched wood.

It was the sprint at the end of the race. She upped the speed, and the bow became a blur. The cord reeled up and down the drill as if bouncing on a pogo stick. There was something clinging to it, she noticed. Attached to the cord. It was hard to see for the motion, but then she realized that it was getting bigger.

One of the strands had frayed! The ends were unwinding even as she watched.

Horrified, she stopped.

The thing was a mess. Little hairs projected, and all of the strands had been damaged.

Before she had a chance to bend the bow and relieve the tension, the cord made a soft tearing noise and parted. The broken ends hung free, twisting like a couple of snakes.

She hurled the ruined bow away. It clattered among the logs. She went to the west, for the sky held a patch of blue in that direction. When she came to the place where the beach ended, she gathered timbers for a raft. The salvaged nails — taken from her pocket and hammered in with a rock — held the cross braces. She paddled the raft along the cliffs until she reached the entrance. Here, the swell of the open sea threatened to break the raft apart beneath her, and she had to land on a patch of shingle.

It was late afternoon. The area of blue beckoned her out to sea, but she could go no farther.

The seaward face of the island was a continuous cliff. The rocks offshore seemed to rise and fall as the breakers swept past. They looked like teeth, worked by a monstrous jaw. Close in, a pair of dark, liquid eyes looked at her from one of the smaller rocks. Then the creature ducked out of sight in the backwash of a wave.

With a weapon — and the will to use it — she could slaughter a sea lion and cut a strip of its hide to make a thong.

That was what she needed. A thong. Either that or a bootlace.

She looked down at her shoes. Soft, sueded leather. Tan. Low-cut. Held on with buckles. Fashionable, too. Very chic this summer, not to have shoelaces.

It was also fashionable to have contoured, specially made jeans. Without anything so crude as a piece of leather to hold them up.

She needed something narrow and limber. She could take a sliver of glass and excise the seam from the side of a trouser leg. Although she'd be forever tripping and falling as a result. Branches and roots would snag the

opening where the seam had been, and that was not to
be taken lightly. A broken leg in this place might prove
fatal.

So using her trousers as a source of material would
have to be a last resort.

A bra strap wouldn't do either. It wouldn't feed smoothly
around the stick. It would abrade at the edges and tear
itself to pieces. What she needed was a cord. Something
smooth. Compact. Strong.

A *cord*.

Not a piece of seaweed like the one below; not the
pounded fibers from a driftwood log; or a red and white
gallon can with the name *Paxco* on it; or a sea-bleached
fragment of surveyor's ribbon, tattered and fragile; or a
strip of wool from her shirt; or a length of orange cotton
from her jacket; or a piece of the plastic lining itself.
None of these things.

Long hair would have done the trick. But her hair was
too short.

The sea lion was back again. She watched the dark,
streamlined head bob about in the surf.

"If I had a strong bow, and a heavy arrow with a
harpoon point, and a length of line, then I might stand
a chance," she told the sea lion. "On second thought . . . if
I had a bow, I'd already have a bowstring, wouldn't I?
Killing you wouldn't be necessary. And in any case, the
bludgeon and the spear are the only options open to me
as a hunter. With patience and luck the best I could do
would be to wound. And then you'd go off where I
couldn't follow, and either you'd die slowly, or else you'd
spend your remaining days as a cripple. Either way, a

stranger would have done you an injury. And to no purpose."

She went down and retrieved the gallon can. At the first sign of movement the sea lion disappeared, this time for good.

Quality Guaranteed, said the can's label. Contains petroleum distillate. Danger! Keep out of the reach of children. Harmful or fatal if swallowed. Read carefully the additional cautionary information on side panel.

She did so, and learned that one was supposed to keep the container tightly closed and its contents away from heat, fire, and open flame.

Trust the Yanks to come up with the right advice at the right moment.

She removed the cap and looked inside. The interior was immaculate, and empty. Which was a pity. A spoonful or two of painter's thinner might have been a help.

There was a ship on the horizon. A freighter. She could see the masts. It occurred to her that the rectangular, silvery bottom of the can might be used to flash a message. Had the sun been shining.

But there was no sun, just the little slice of blue, off to the west. The ship was too far away in any case.

9

By morning, the sky had changed. Instead of a deck of gray stratus, there came a rushing mass of cumulus clouds. They bumbled along at low altitude like a herd of cotton elephants, stampeded by the wind. Patches of early morning sunlight swept across the mountains and along the beach. Shadow one moment, sun the next.

She had awakened with a feeling of hope. Although the experiments with firemaking had come to naught, she was still better off than before, thanks to the empty thinner can. Properly used, the tin could increase her chance of being rescued, for even if the shipping lanes were too distant, a beam of reflected sunlight could hardly be missed by someone a short distance off in a low-flying plane.

The can would have to be modified, however.

She took one of her salvaged nails — it was almost heavy enough to be called a spike — and with repeated blows from a stone, she shaped its malleable iron into a chisel point. With this, she removed the bottom of the can, driving her makeshift chisel centimeter by centimeter around the edge, using a piece of root as a mallet. She ended up with a flat, rectangular mirror measuring perhaps fifteen centimeters by ten. The mirror was stiffened at its edge by the remnant of a seam where the sides of the can had been attached.

Again using her chisel, she punched a hole two centimeters across exactly in the center of the mirror. The hole was for sighting; if the mirror was to be a reliable signaling device, the narrow beam of reflected sunlight had to be aimed.

While waiting for the sun to make one of its random appearances, she practiced the technique. Holding the mirror to her eye with one hand and extending the other hand in front of her, she could look through the hole and see her upraised forefinger. The idea was to tilt the mirror so that a patch of brightness lighted the end of your finger. This told you precisely where the beam was going. To signal in Morse, you simply nodded your head. This brought the spot of reflected sunlight down where you could see it on your arm — away from the target — thus creating the interval between flashes.

The device had a limited arc of effectiveness, as she soon discovered during a break in the clouds. The quivering rectangle of light was quite distinct whenever she chose a target within a hundred and twenty degrees of the sun. If the angle grew much greater than that, however, the beam was narrow and weak.

She noticed something else, whenever the bright patch

of light touched her hand. The metal mirror was handling more than just the visible spectrum of the sun's rays. It was reflecting heat as well.

The idea hit her so suddenly it was like a jolt of electricity.

Solar oven.

Fire wasn't the only way food could be cooked! She should have thought of it earlier. It was such an obvious use of the can's gleaming interior!

Looking in through the open end, she began to visualize how the thing might be done. First the top would have to be cut off, then the seam along the side. The resulting sheet of metal could then be shaped into a smooth curve.

The device was completed in record time. Two sections of plank held the sheet, top and bottom; the whole affair being supported by a mound of sand and oriented toward the point in the sky where the sun would next appear. "The Pig Trough Oven," she chuckled, giving the metal a last polish with her shirt sleeve. On impulse, she went to the clam reserve, smashed open several shells, wrapped what she could around a stick, and ran back to the reflector with it.

The beach was beginning to brighten. She held the stick crossways to the device. When the sun came, extremely brilliant slashes and stars of light appeared along the sides of the stick. The clam flesh became translucent, glowing like a strip of film in a projector. She moved the stick up and down to locate the mirror's focal point. The effect was spotty and uneven. At the center of one of the star-shaped areas, where the light was brightest, there was enough heat to bring water to a boil. She could hear an occasional hiss, and from time to time a small bubble appeared. But the areas of greatest heat made up only a small fraction of the total area. Elsewhere, there was only enough heat to make things warm — too warm for her hand, but not hot enough for cooking. The aberrations of the mirror were too great. Exact focusing was impossible.

There was no method of containing the heat radiated away, either.

She experimented with the signal mirror, holding it above the stick and trying to reflect a few of the scattered rays back on their target.

No dice.

The thing couldn't be done. The reflective area was too small for cooking. In addition, the single sheet of metal could only be deformed along one axis at a time. The reflector was, in effect, part of a cylinder and was focused along an extended locus rather than upon a single point. What she needed was a reflector shaped something like the end of an egg.

A paraboloid.

She sat contemplating the device. "Useless pig trough!" she said. She dug the stick into the sand. "Science triumphs again!"

"Well," commented the voice of Reason, "what did you expect? Things are always more complex than they look. And that goes for the simple technologies also."

It would have been more satisfying just to throw the

thing away, as she had the bow. But instead, she lifted the piece of metal carefully from the sand. She took it over to a flat plank, and hammered a notch in the edge of the metal, using the chisel point of the nail. She positioned the sheet so the notched edge was even with the side of the plank before placing a piece of board on top.

She stood on the board.

Gripping the protruding flap of sheet metal with a folded piece of cedar bark — to protect her fingers from the razorlike edge — she gave a hard, upward pull, tearing the sheet in half.

The newly shorn edge, as expected, began at the place where she'd notched the sheet. It followed the contour of the board she'd been standing on for most of its length, curving outward only at the end.

Ignoring the imperfection of it, she took the two half sheets and tore each of them into six smaller pieces, using the same technique as before. When she was done, there were twelve long triangles.

The pointed ends curled, like springs.

She straightened these out, and punched a single hole in each of the twelve triangles, right at the apex.

With the chisel nail, she drilled a hole into the end grain of a branch, and pinned all twelve of the metal triangles in place, driving a tapered twig through the twelve openings in the metal and down into the single hole at the end of the branch.

She hammered the twig deeper into the hole. This held everything tight. Then she arranged the triangles in a pinwheel. Taking this somewhat bizarre creation into the middle of the beach, she planted it firmly in the sand. It stood shoulder high, looking like a small windmill, except the blades were tilted toward the sun.

Bending each blade into a smooth curve with her fingers, she soon destroyed all resemblance to a windmill. The thing now looked like a large metal flower: a tulip. The petals of the tulip were silvery inside; they glinted in the sun. The outside was a patchwork of lettering, left over from the tulip's former existence as a container. Across one petal, in large red letters, was the word DANGER!

Smiling at this, she went to find a wooden sliver of the correct size.

The sun was still shining when she returned. With the splinter, she began probing the reflector's interior. As it approached the center, the little spear of cedar glowed with concentrated light. The glare was so intense she had to slit her eyes against it, and even then it was painful.

Other than this, nothing happened.

Perhaps the main area of focus was farther down.

She probed deeper, squinting against the light. It happened so quickly she had no time to react. As the point of the sliver descended, there came a sizzling sound, and the inside of the reflector filled with smoke. Instinctively, she shut her eyes, for in the center the smoke glowed with a ferocious white light. There was a hollow *poof.* An instant later she felt a stinging sensation on the tip of her finger where it held the sliver.

"Ouch!"

The remains of the sliver now lay on the sand, blackened and smoking.

Save for the portion held between her fingers, ignition had evidently been instantaneous along its entire length. Which was understandable. All of the wood inside the reflector had been preheated, and the explosive puffing sound must have been what firemen refer to as flashover: particles of smoke, catching all at once.

"I'm going to have to find a longer sliver," she mused.

It was difficult to believe — this silly-looking tulip actually worked!

She was collecting the kindling and the firewood when she had to stop, look back, and assure herself that the thing truly existed.

Out on the sand, the reflector seemed more like a tulip than ever, swaying on the end of its stalk in the wind.

10

As must have occurred thousands of years before, when the first hearth-keeper tended the first fire, there came a new cohesion to the various tasks of the day. Her interactions with this creature called fire were akin to those of a marriage — at least in some ways. In others, it was like caring for a child. She made offerings of dry wood, and in return the fire cooked her food, helped in making tools, kept rain and cold and darkness at bay. But a fire needed more than fuel. It needed guarding, and this confined most of her other activities to one location. No longer was it possible for her to sleep in one place, store food in another, keep salvage in a third, and do her crafting of tools and artifacts in yet another spot a hundred meters away. Fire was a magnet to all of these things. There was a reason why the word "hearth" was a synonym for "home." Fire demanded that it be the focus of all activity. Not only that; it was sedentary. You couldn't pick it up and carry it around with you, as you could a child. And you could never, never allow it to walk on its own.

That was another of its demands. The selection of a *place* had to be made with the requirements of fire in mind.

She chose the ledge at the base of the pinnacle, which proved to be nearly ideal. Burning on a rocky surface, her fire could never creep out of control. It was also above the level of the sand, which had been a constant nuisance before, always showing up where it wasn't wanted. A meter and a half away stood the divan-shaped rock. The pool of water at its lower end now did double duty: she could keep clams in it as before, or, by dropping in fire-heated stones, convert the hollow in the rock into a caldron of boiling water.

Even when the tide was in, and cold salt water filled the space between her cooking rock and the pinnacle, there was no inconvenience. She could hop from rock to ledge and back again with little risk. Access to the mainland was along the ledge and through the arching tunnel of logs. The tunnel was much too drafty and damp to convert into a shelter for herself, but it made a good shelter for the main supply of firewood. The larger chunks weren't hurt by an occasional drop of water; only the tinder and kindling needed to be kept completely dry.

Her primary shelter was constructed to seaward of the fire, where the ledge was at its widest. Here, the wall of the pinnacle was slightly concave, providing an overhanging roof. Between the roof and the ledge she erected a palisade of branches, wedging them in place, top and

bottom. Crossways to the vertical branches, she interlaced a set of horizontal ones, to form a grille. To this
she secured an overlapping thatch of umbrella leaves
from the marsh, starting at the bottom, as in shingling a
roof, and tying the leaves stem uppermost to the frame
with strips of cedar bark.

When they were all in place, the leaves looked like
the scales of a large green fish.

Not long after, a brief but torrential rain disclosed a
flaw in her arrangements. The rain, driven against the
cliff by the wind, flowed down the rock and under
the moss caulking she'd used, relentlessly cascading along
the inside of the frame.

The remedy came about through the kindly assistance
of the fire. She took a flat stone, heated it, and placed
lumps of pitch on top. When melted, the pitch ran like
honey, and she was able to glue strips of umbrella leaf
directly to the rock with it. The pitch also made a wa-
tertight seal. The strips of leaf overlapped the shelter
wall like lengths of flashing at the peak of a roof, and
when the next rainstorm came, the shelter proved at last
to be worthy of the name.

Still, refinements were needed. Her little house gaped
at both ends. When the wind was from the wrong direction, smoke from the fire poured through the structure
as if it were a chimney. She put an end to this by building
a removable hatch to block off the southern end of the
shelter. This cut down on the draft, allowing her to enjoy
the heat of the fire through the opening on the landward
side without suffering the smoke. Having designed the

hatch so it would open easily, she retained access to the area beyond, even during those times when the beach was under water.

Access was important, for her supplies of food were stored along the outer ledge — or, more accurately, above the ledge. At first glance it would have seemed a curious arrangement, this net of woven vines hanging against the cliff. It was her larder, held in place with strips of bark which had been glued directly to the rock with pitch. A bonnet of leaves protected her provender from sun and rain, and the whole affair was reachable only by standing on tiptoe.

The animals responsible for these elaborate precautions had made their presence known during the first week. Her inventory of clams in the storage pool kept running short, and at first she suspected the gulls of gliding in and stealing from her when she wasn't looking. It soon became apparent, however, that the clams were disappearing only at night, when the gulls weren't flying. This coincided with the time when small, handlike prints were being left in the sand. There were new ones each morning.

Evidently, she was dealing with a family of raccoons.

It was probably more of a game for them in the beginning. Had the animals been able to open the shells on their own, they would have cleaned her out then and there, instead of contenting themselves with two or three a night.

With the appearance of *cooked* clams, however — clams that had been steamed, taken from their shells, dehydrated, and smoked — the game began to be played in earnest. There were four of these bandits, and they grew amazingly bold. Even in daylight, she saw rounded, bear-like forms the size of a terrier ghosting about. She felt under siege. She couldn't let anything edible out of her sight; either it would be gone when she turned around, or else she'd find herself facing an obstinate raccoon — eye on food and reluctant to give ground. There was a large one in particular, whom she named Scipio Afri-canus, after an ancient Roman general. Scipio would hiss and emit throaty, quacking sounds. But he was not a very brave general, and always led the retreat whenever she advanced and used her voice.

What was puzzling was that the raccoons continued to steal, even after the meaty items were placed beyond their reach. She'd dug up a number of sword ferns, washed the roots, sliced them into chunks, and roasted the chunks like potatoes, in jackets of seaweed. Cooked in this way, the root of the sword fern was, as Pauline had described, perfectly good to eat. It had a pleasant, nutty flavor, and was a welcome addition to a diet that had formerly con-sisted of almost pure protein. For some reason, the nor-mally carnivorous raccoons seemed to have a taste for it also; as a result, the pieces of broiled sword fern root soon joined the smoked clams in the aerial larder.

After a week of privation, the act of storing food was a marvel to her. Fire, shelter, food — all were luxuries now. True, she'd have given almost anything for a set of fresh clothing, a hot bath, a clean towel, or a hairbrush. But for all that, her spirits rose. Even the onset of rainy weather had little effect on her growing optimism. She had her umbrella leaf hat to protect her head against the rain, and she had her warm jacket, and her fire, and plenty to eat, and a dry place to sleep. And sooner or later, help would come.

In the middle of the second week, when the shelter was finished, she went and retrieved the raft at the western end of the beach. Ever since that frustrating afternoon of the broken cord, it had lain undisturbed beneath a pile of stones — a crude method of mooring, but effective. Off-loading the stone ballast, she took the raft and made a voyage with it to Whale Rock.

It was eerie, setting foot on that fateful chunk of stone for the second time. She found the scraped place among the acorn barnacles where the little death trap of a raft had been launched ten days before. Higher up, where there were no barnacles, the marks left by the plane were more difficult to see, having been darkened by repeated lavings of the tide. The shards of metal, however, were still bright. She recovered every scrap, and when she was through, the pocket of the jacket had a definite heft to it. Last of all, she took the board she was using as a paddle and pried the aluminum cap from its knob of rock. Holding the metal shell up to the light, she could see no openings. It would make a good cup.

The purpose of the expedition had been to gather aluminum scrap. With a hundred grams or so at her disposal, she might be able to melt the aluminum down and cast herself a spoon or a fork. The idea had a certain elegance. Imagine having such an artifact! It would be a fascinating memento, and would prove just how much a person could do under primitive conditions.

Her mind was filled with pleasant speculation about this. First, she imagined an open mold of fired clay, within which the aluminum could be melted. Then another idea attracted her. If the mold itself could be placed in the fire to melt down the chips of metal, wouldn't it also be possible to make a *crucible* of clay? There would be a crust of oxide and other impurities floating on the surface of the molten metal. If one used a separate container for the melting, all the dross could be removed first, and only the pure metal would go into the mold.

With great enthusiasm, she searched the face of the bluff for a usable deposit of clay. The project, however, went no further than this, for during her search she uncovered something far more valuable than potter's clay.

It was a stone. A fairly average stone, perhaps two kilograms in weight: flat and more or less trapezoidal in shape. The thing was valueless by itself, but over the years it had managed to stay in precisely the right position while the root of a tree grew around it. She worked with her chisel nail to cut the root at the treeward end, leaving a handle still attached to the stone.

It was a Neanderthal's dream — the perfect implement for bashing things.

Stone and root were united inseparably. The hatchet-shaped head was not the right material for fashioning an edge, but this didn't matter. She used the thing as a maul for making firewood, and in this role alone, the Bashing Tool, as she came to call it, saved her hours of work every day. The time spent in food gathering was also shortened. Instead of using a stick to laboriously scrape a trench around the base of a sword fern, and then severing the innumerable rootlets from the main root with a small, hand-held stone, she could now flail away with Bashing Tool, accomplishing as much in ten minutes as had taken forty, earlier.

She had by now decided that the making of an aluminum artifact could not be justified, however appealing the idea might be. She didn't need a spoon. The energy spent in making such a thing would be an investment in pride, not in practicality. It would be a foolish bauble for show and tell: a waste of valuable time.

Rather than experiment with crucibles and molds, she built a squat framework of wood. It was shaped like a birdcage. The rounded dome reached no higher than her knee, but it still took a great deal of work. The interlaced branches had to be securely lashed together, for if the device were to function, the joins needed to resist a crushing action similar to that of a powerful vise.

Beneath the dome went a stout, removable floor, also made of branches. None of the openings in either the dome or the floor of the cage was large enough to permit the escape of anything larger than a Ping-Pong ball.

Next, she cut a doorway in the side of the structure, about twenty centimeters in width. Across the opening she suspended a small door, hinged at the top with loops made from a scrap of barbed wire. The door was counterbalanced. When pushed from the outside, the door opened inward and one could reach inside the cage.

Withdraw the hand, and the stone weight of the coun-
terbalance automatically swung the door shut.

A creature pushing from the inside would not be able
to get out.

There remained one problem: What would be the best
way of lowering the trap into the water?

In the end she gave up the idea of a line entirely. Crab
fishermen used a line because they needed an up-haul
adaptable to various depths. If she decided on a depth
in advance, she could then use a rigid up-haul, such as
a long branch. This could be fastened securely to the
top of the cage and would float upright in the water, with
the top just below tide level. In this way, the action of
the waves wouldn't be transmitted to the tethered structure on the bottom. A wooden bobber could be tied to
the end of the branch with a length of vine. The bobber
would then serve to mark the position of the trap.

She chose a depth of three fathoms (three times the
length of her outstretched arms) and once the trap was
in place, the wooden marker appeared on the surface of
the bay at every low tide. Daily, she paddled out, positioned the raft above the bobber, and reached down
into the water to grasp the end of the submerged pole.
Pulling in the trap, hand over hand, was always a time
of suspense. Ashore, there was water in the cooking pool,
and a pile of stones ready to heat, and a large reserve of
firewood — all in the hope of finding a dungeness crab
in the trap. She could see the way it would happen,
down below. The creature would sidle into the current,
following the scent of the bait inside the cage. He would

crawl up the framework, exploring here and there. Gripping with his pincers. Pushing. Until at last a section of the barrier gave way . . .

But the trap continued to come up empty, except for the ballast of stones and the bait of crushed barnacles. Every day she went out in the raft to check the trap. Disappointed, she would replace the old bait with freshly broken barnacles and return the cage to the bottom.

11

She dreamt of a cabin built of logs. It rested on pilings, sunk vertically into the marsh so that the cabin stood high in the air, as if on stilts. This was a protection against . . . some threat or other. She couldn't remember what.

From the front door, a gangway angled toward the beach, and in the dream she walked down the gangway. Winter had come, and it was cold. She had to push her way through heavy snow as she went, and the gangway rebounded underfoot like a weighted trampoline. When she got to the beach, she began digging for clams. The sand underneath the snow was hard with frost and mixed with the ashes of an ancient fire. Clams were nowhere to be found. There were only the clocks. Hundreds upon hundreds of rusted clocks.

She was awakened from the dream by the sniffing of an animal. Opening her eyes, she found Scipio Africanus peeking in at her, his masked face appearing just above the contour of the ledge.

"Good morning, Scipio," she said.

At the sound of her voice, the raccoon vanished. There was a scurrying noise from below, and after a moment, Scipio Africanus could be seen galumphing along the beach, followed by two of his cohorts. They presently disappeared among the driftwood.

Racoons were mostly nocturnal, but there was only an hour or two of true darkness here during the summer solstice. They wouldn't have enough darkness in which to do their foraging and would have to go out whether it was daytime or not.

The sky, she noted, was its customary gray this morning. But at least it wasn't raining. She got up and removed the small lean-to of planks that sheltered the fire. There was nothing showing on the surface; only a fine powder of ash, holding the shape of what had been pieces of firewood hours earlier. She held out a hand to find the warmth, then bent over and breathed on it. The ash disintegrated to reveal a bed of coals below. She tucked a few wisps of dry grass among the coals and, when this flared, added a handful of twigs. Broken pieces of stick followed the twigs, then still larger pieces, until a merry blaze licked upward against the rock.

She warmed herself, and steam rose from her clothing as the dampness of the night was driven off. The process was speeded by taking off the jacket and drying it separately. The same for the shoes and stockings. She sat and toasted the soles of her feet before the fire while the stockings hung on a stick nearby. For perhaps the fourth time in as many days she considered finding a block of wood, so she'd be able to sit at the fire with greater dignity and comfort. And just as she had on the other occasions, she decided against it. The ledge was already crowded; a stool-sized block would merely be another thing for her to trip over. She'd fall in the drink some evening when the tide was in — though, come to think of it, the possibility that this would happen over the next few days was exactly zero. The neaps had arrived: the tides were neither very high nor very low. If she'd tumbled off the ledge last night she would have hit dry sand, for at high tide the water hadn't even gone as far as the foot of Cooking Rock.

Her mind shifted from the trivial to the practical. The subject of the tide had brought up a matter of more immediate concern. For the next several days she'd have to depend entirely on the reserves of meat in the larder. (Unless, of course, a crab turned up in the trap.) The clam beds would still be covered at low tide, so she wouldn't be able . . .

So *that* was it!

Her memory of the dream had begun to fade, but she could still remember the essentials. Winter, a cabin on stilts, no clams. There were a few disturbing elements, but these were illogical and could be dismissed. The source of the whole thing was the fact that the neaps had arrived and she wouldn't be digging any more clams for a while. That was all the dream was saying. The brooding, frightening aspects had no meaning. None at all.

"And anyway," she reminded herself, "I've got a treat for breakfast this morning." The evening before, she'd picked a handful of dandelion buds — not the flowers themselves, but the small, soft lumps that showed just before the flowers opened. The recipe for dandelion omelette involved such things as eggs, milk, onions, butter, salt, pepper — and an omelette pan — none of which she possessed. The important thing to note, of course, was that dandelion buds were *edible*. She would just have to do without the rest of it.

In preparation, she scooped a mound of coals into a hollow in the rock. She poured a little water into her aircraft-aluminum cup, then bedded the cup among the coals. When the water boiled, she dumped in the buds and covered the cup with a lid of bark to trap the steam. The cup simmered atop the coals.

It would have been pleasant to be able to brew some tea. She knew where there was a stand of Labrador tea — at least the plants *looked* like Labrador tea. But that was the problem. There was a variety known as false Labrador tea, very similar in appearance. Make an infusion of one, and you had an enjoyable drink with breakfast. Brew up with the leaves of the other and you had a cup of poison.

She improvised a song about it:

> *Poison, poison, drink it up!*
> *Chill of winter in the cup!*

And there it was again. That silly dream about clocks and winter! What was the matter with her? The whole thing had been ridiculous. A cabin on *stilts,* for heaven's sake!

Irritated with herself, she put on her shoes and went

to get a leaf-wrapped breakfast ration from the larder. When she returned, she lifted the piece of bark to see how the dandelions were doing. The water had turned slightly greenish, but when she prodded the buds with a splinter they still seemed underdone. She put the cover back and chewed on a piece of dehydrated clam.

Snow on the ground and nothing to eat.

Dreams had a crazy logic of their own at times. Take the idea of a cabin. If she were to stay here through the winter, that was what she would need: a small cabin. A rocky ledge and a campfire wouldn't do — not at fifty-three degrees north latitude — not with twenty hours of darkness out of every twenty-four during the months of December and January. In addition to the cabin she'd need enormous supplies of firewood, properly broken up. She'd need winter clothing. Bedding. Food — four or five months' worth of food.

It was quite impossible. She lacked the resources, the equipment, the knowledge. Above all, she lacked the *time*.

A solitary human equipped with Stone Age tools would not be able to accomplish all that needed to be done. A group of people might succeed. A dozen pairs of hands: chopping, clearing, carrying, weaving, fishing, trapping, skinning, tanning, smoking, digging, building.

Eighteen, twenty hours a day.

A dozen pairs of hands to raise the shelter and break up fuel for the fire — and all would share the shelter and the fire. With only one person, there would be nearly as much work, as far as shelter and heating were concerned, but only one pair of hands, not twelve.

Survive the winter alone? She wouldn't have a chance. The clams were only going to last through September, maybe into October, but after that?

For the first time that morning, she looked at the platform she'd built. The little table of logs rested atop the driftwood, covered with a protective layer of sand. Above the sand was a pile of dry brush, ready for lighting. And above that was a layer of greenery, to create smoke.

On the ledge beside her was a creation that looked something like a medieval broom. It was a quick-lighting torch to carry the flame from the campfire over to the mound of brush on the platform.

She decided to try an experiment. What did the theoreticians call it? A thought experiment? When it was simply imagined?

Yes. A thought experiment.

She imagined what it would be like, hearing the sound of a piston-engined aircraft. She imagined how long it would take for her to identify the sound, and to react.

She began counting seconds aloud.

It would take eight seconds before she could reasonably be expected to pick up the torch. At the count of nine, the torch would be in the fire. By the count of twelve, the flame would have taken hold.

In her mind's eye she saw herself running across the sand. By the count of eighteen, the tinder beneath the pile of brush would begin to catch. By the count of thirty, the flames would be licking among the piled vines and green leaves, but as yet smoke would not have risen. There'd be only a thin white streamer here and there.

It would take an absolute minimum of forty-five seconds, she concluded, before she'd have a decent column of smoke. That was much too long. Say the plane came over the mountains to the south, approaching from across the bay — the very best case. By the time the smoke began to rise the plane would already be overhead, and a few seconds later it would have flown across the mountain to the north and out of sight.

As with the signal mirror, the conditions would have to be precisely right. The aircraft would have to be flying slowly. It would have to come from the south. It would have to pass a kilometer or so to the side, rather than directly overhead. And yet, it would have to be within two kilometers of the pinnacle or the MAYDAY signal would be illegible. If the plane was much farther away, the eyes of the people aboard might be drawn toward the smoke, but they would have no way of identifying it as a distress signal. Without the word MAYDAY, the white tendril from her fire would be just another of the innumerable plumes of smoke to be seen along the coast.

Smoke from campfires. From fishing villages. From the burning of slash at logging camps.

And another thing:

The plane couldn't pass to the *east* of the pinnacle, because the MAYDAY signal was on a slab of rock that tilted to the west. In order for her signaling system to work, a plane would have to fly along a narrow corridor measuring perhaps a kilometer in width. The aircraft would already be at an altitude of at least a thousand meters to clear the mountains; but if it was much above two or three thousand, she might as well forget it.

Unless, of course, the sun was shining from exactly

the right quarter. Then those people in the plane would notice!

She looked down at the signal mirror. It hung like a giant dog tag from her neck, supported by its failed-bowstring of a necklace. The thing went everywhere with her; she'd even learned to wear it while sleeping.

OK, my fine-feathered, thought-experimenter friend, what's the conclusion? Is it possible?

"It's possible," she said, answering her own question. "*Barely* possible."

Except she hadn't seen any planes. Not for two weeks.

There had been that twin-engined something-or-other that first day, but she'd never actually *seen* it. Ever since then, she had assumed there would be others.

But there hadn't been.

The plane had probably been on its way to help with the search. Off to the south. Where radio contact had been lost; where everyone had been looking.

Mister — what was his name? Tate? — liked to keep a close watch on his planes. That's what Jim had said. If a plane didn't report on schedule, Tate would know exactly where to look. Only this time the procedure had backfired. The plane had been in the air a long time after the radio failed; they'd been a hundred kilometers and more to the north before going down.

And by now the search would have been called off. Missing and presumed dead. Case closed.

We do sympathize, Doctor Bradbury. About your daughter. Really we do. But you must realize that the resources of the provincial government are *appallingly* limited. Two more light planes have gone missing since this one. As of last report, a hundred and forty-two hours of flight time have been logged on this one effort. And nothing has turned up. No radio beacon. No debris. Nothing.

She lifted the cover of bark from the aluminum cup. The water had mostly evaporated, leaving the dandelions lying dark and limp at the bottom. She speared one of them with her sliver, and blew on it. The yellow part of the flower could be seen inside.

Not too bad, she concluded, taking a bite.

Tangy.

They had a flavor similar to that of spinach . . . could have used a little salt. She'd try simmering them in sea water next time.

12

Take a strake of lumber. Lay it on the ground. And beside it lay another.

Bevel the edges where they touch. Then shave the edges down so the two planks taper at each end. Lying together now, they're like the forked tongue of a dragon, no matter which end is viewed — the bow or the stern.

Bend the planks up and inward so the separated ends join together. And lo! The two planks form a slender trough, curving gracefully upward — at bow and stern.

Carve a keel to fit, and fasten the keel to the planks to hold them together, and extend the keel so it rises beyond the bottom strakes. These extensions thus become a pair of lifted arms — *here* the stem, *there* the sternpost.

Pair by pair, add the strakes: filling out the bottom, rounding out the bilges. The planks are neatly fitted to the posts; they may either overlap the planks below or lie beside, flush and smooth. Whichever — clinker-built or caravel — the sides rise up. Layer by layer, the ends of the vessel climb along the posts until she forms a crescent moon, full-bellied, but pointed in the places where the water will be cut.

Within lie the ribs. Some are bent in place, others trimmed to fit inside the shell. And in this ancient style of building, the ribs don't always run the distance from the keel to the rail. They're a patchwork. An afterthought. A method of keeping the strakes from sliding, one against the other: not a rigid frame as in vessels built today. The boat doesn't have a framework. It is a shell, growing from the ground into a shape to please the builder's eye, just as the soft clay rises on the potter's wheel.

Stiffening comes later.

At least, such had been the practice long ago. The prehistoric trading ships had all been crafted to this rule — first the planking, then the ribs — even the fleets of Egypt, and of Rome.

Such a vessel needed far less timber, and the fastenings were smaller. This appealed to her, just as it had to the shipwrights of old. Given a choice, she would have preferred a lapstraked vessel, such as the Norsemen built. Pressure from the water underneath would have helped to hold it together. The ribs would have been secured with lashings to small cleats chiseled out of the inside of the strakes, and the boat would have been very flexible.

But she knew it to be wishful thinking. That old nemesis, the lack of proper metal, rose to block the way. Aluminum was too soft to hold an edge; she couldn't use it to create either ripsaw or carpenter's plane. Both were essential. To build a boat in the Viking style, one would need a saw to cut the long planks, and a plane to smooth the edges where one plank met another, for with such a vessel the seams would have to be perfectly made.

She had a number of driftwood planks, of course. These came in every size imaginable, but it would still be possible for her to construct a bargelike vessel with them: slab-sided, the end and bottom pieces running athwartship. But the structure would need to be pegged together, and that would be its weakness. In the finished barge, the simple act of resting her knee on one of the bottom planks could pull out the pegs that held it in place.

Like opening a door in the bottom of the boat.

There might be a way around the problem, but she wanted nothing to do with a barge. It would be heavy and slow, with little freeboard, and no sheer. The vessel would be incapable of lifting to the swell. In short, it would be a coffin, both in appearance and in function; suitable for crossing a pond, perhaps, but not for the open sea.

She could visualize clearly what it was going to be like — this trip of forty or fifty nautical miles — with a hostile, rocky coast to leeward. It made her wish for the fleet little Thistle resting in its cradle back home. *Mary Shelley*, with her planing hull and efficient rig, would have made short work of such a passage. How ironic: to think that at the end of the voyage there would be yet another Thistle, almost identical to *Shelley*. Another little sloop. Her father had rented it for the summer, in the hope that it would give her pleasure while she was with him at the dig.

But there was little profit in thinking of that. The

vessel that would carry her to her father's camp would have to be *built*. Here. With her own hands. And before the work could start, a number of decisions had to be made.

Design decisions.

The distance to be covered wasn't great. But it would require the proper equipment.

And there was the rub. Proper equipment meant a vessel light enough to ride the swell; high enough to avoid shipping water; strong enough to hold together, no matter what the state of the sea; tight enough to leak only a small amount; and, on top of all this, lean and swift enough to cover the distance in a reasonable length of time solely under the power of her two arms.

One thing was certain: the techniques of the Iron Age did not apply. As her father might have put it, Welcome to the Neolithic.

Say farewell to metal, and to all that it implies. Forget the caulked seams and the elegantly contoured strakes. *This* was the world of fire and stone, of animal fat and whalebone.

Welcome to the Neolithic.

Welcome to the restrictions of *place*. To the confinement of a particular locality. The wood of the balsa tree would not make a seagoing raft for *her*. Not here. That was the rule — that was the limitation of the Neolithic. One was restricted by what could be found nearby. No other options allowed.

But for all that, she was still fortunate. Extremely so!

The forests of the province held a treasure called the cedar. Large-trunked: soft-wooded. The older trees had a heartwood as dark and rich as smoked salmon. And like the salmon, the cedar was made for the sea. The ancient peoples knew this, the Haida and the others, and from the cedar they had crafted their canoes. Magnificent, seagoing canoes. Carved from a single massive trunk.

She too would build a boat of cedar, she decided. And fire would be her tool.

13

The day of the two fires began with a heavy fog. Early on that gray morning she went along the beach to the place where she'd emerged from the forest the time of the grizzly. Here, a portion of the bluff had collapsed years before, taking a medium-sized cedar with it. The roots of the tree were at the level of the beach; the branches lay at an angle in the forest. Between, there was a section of trunk free of branches, measuring more than a pace in diameter and seven paces in length — the overall dimensions of the boat to be.

Having brought live coals with her, she now built a pair of fires underneath the log: one down near the roots, the other up at the lip of the bluff. Once the log was burned to length, it would be possible for her to lever it across the barrier of driftwood on a bridge of timber. From there, she could roll the thing down the shingle to the water and float it back to camp.

More easily said than done. Burning a tree in two isn't a trifling task, especially when the trunk is over a meter across and not quite dry. She'd brought Bashing Tool along, and that was a help. Scrambling back and forth from fire to fire, she knocked away the developing layers of charcoal, exposing fresh wood to the flames. The displaced charcoal helped in feeding the fires below, but didn't provide enough fuel to keep the flames working upon the trunk. So there were endless trips for firewood.

The work was grueling. By midmorning she felt as if she'd put in a full day already. And yet the contour of the trunk had hardly been altered. Exasperating though it was, she kept on with it, for the task *had* to be done.

The fog lifted after a while and the sun came out, adding its own heat to that of the fires. She took a break at noon, allowing the fires to tend themselves while she ate a lunch of smoked clams and newly ripened berries. There was also broiled thistle root, but it was not very palatable.

The sound might have gone unnoticed had she been working. As it was, she heard it after taking a swallow of water.

She replaced the cap on the bottle and went down to the bay, listening. The plane, she noted, was somewhere to the west, while the sun was to the south: the angle was therefore well within the limit. She got out the mirror, tested the position to be certain she had it right, and then lowered the device so she'd have both eyes for locating the plane.

As before, the engine noise came from beyond the headlands, traveling from north to south. But it sounded like a plane with only one engine this time, not two.

And it was more distant. It paralleled the coast, several kilometers offshore. Traveling very fast.

It came, and then it went, and the bay was silent once more. The thing might as well have been a ghost of an airplane, for it had been invisible to her the whole time.

She dropped the mirror and let it dangle on its cord. Slowly, she went back to work. She fed the fires and pounded charcoal from the hollows. The sap buzzed and whistled as it turned to steam inside the tree. By mid-afternoon, she'd finished the last of the water. She felt oiled with sweat. Near the upper fire, a piece of rotten log began to smolder. There were holes in the log, and from out of the holes ran a black flood of large ants. They tumbled over one another, falling down the bluff toward the main fire. The heat seemed to drive them insane. They dashed about, their momentum at times carrying them too close to the source of their torment, so that the legs burned off and a legion of squirming shapes hissed and popped among the ashes.

She stopped work to watch.

Above the burning city of the ants was a dry branch, projecting past the edge of the bluff. The branch caught fire, and after a time ignited a patch of grass. She moved to extinguish the grass fire . . . but it was as if the movement was resisted by an invisible hand. Something held her back.

The grass burned. Above, the dried stalks of an ancient briar began to shrivel and sway in the current of super-heated air, shimmering upward in the sunlight.

She hadn't thought of it before.

It simply had not occurred to her, although it ought to have been obvious. Here was a signal she could have made right from the beginning. Right from the moment she first kindled a fire.

Her imprisonment was an illusion. *She had it in her power to send a signal they couldn't possibly ignore.*

Planes would come. And men. Parachutists, with shovels in their hands and spray cans on their backs. The province had an army of fire fighters, ready to spring into action at a moment's notice.

All they needed was word of a fire. A *large* fire.

The idea seemed, in that instant, to be the most logical, the most appropriate, the most efficient solution to a problem ever to be conceived.

It was satisfying. It was right. It was an example of sheer mind-power, triumphant over a world of indifference and hardship and injustice.

It was brilliance.

More: it was genius.

It was a thing for which the hands were clasped and raised above the head.

It was . . . utter folly: a stupidity so gross that the memory of it, hours later, brought her to a stand in the twilight.

Her shirt had a hole burned in it. She was covered with filth. An unpleasant odor contaminated the coolness of the evening — her hair had been singed.

How could she have been so witless?

There had been a terrible moment when the side of a tree had gone up in a roaring tower of flame. She'd known then what the thing she had created would be like. It was as if the cries of a thousand guiltless creatures had blended with the sound of the dying tree, as its resinous vapor exploded and the incandescent twigs and needles whirled upward.

She'd seen how it would be.

The top of one tree would explode below another, and in seconds the foliage of the next would go up, igniting two more. The fire would leap upward, climbing the steep side of the mountain faster than even a deer could run. It would be a crown fire, the most dreaded of all fires. The creatures caught in it would have no chance.

And some of them might be men.

Fire fighters, summoned by one Elly Bradbury.

They'd try to hold the ridges. In places their line would hold, in others it wouldn't. Surrounded, trapped by the very forest they had come to save, they would have no escape.

But at least she'd caught it in time. The mistake had been redeemed. Every glowing spark had at last been hunted down. Every blackened fragment had been taken to the water and drowned. Objects too large to move, such as the log itself, had been thoroughly drenched with hundreds upon hundreds of plastic bottle loads of salt water. In the places where water couldn't reach, she'd used applications of wet clay.

The thing was out. It was dead. There wasn't a single wisp of smoke . . . anywhere.

With infinite weariness, she stumbled home along the beach. Reaching the tiny spring, she was about to kneel and drink when she caught sight of Scipio Africanus and his band. The four of them went humpety-humpety along the ledge and into the tunnel. A moment later she could see them climbing the bluff, headed for their den within the forest.

The thought came to her of how it might have ended for them. She saw the little family forced from cover, amid the glare and the heat from above. She saw them running with their fur alight, with nowhere to go. And seeing it, she wept as she'd never wept before.

14

There came a morning when the great round of cedar rested at last near the top of the beach, halfway between Cooking Rock and the spring. At high tide the evening before, she'd moored the log above the ends of two wooden rails. Now, with the tide out, the log sat atop the rails looking formidably large.

With much straining at levers and wedges, she rolled the log up this makeshift railway and set it in position on a pair of keel blocks, beyond the reach of the tide. She had just enough room to squeeze past, between the log and the barrier of driftwood above.

By midmorning, fifty wooden pegs — twenty-five to a side — had been pounded like spikes into the soft wood. End-on, the timber appeared to have sprouted a pair of stubby picket fences, marking out the upper third of the log. Freshly stripped of its bark, the wood showed an occasional crack between one peg and another, and wherever these cracks appeared, she drove in additional pegs.

Soon the cracks lengthened and joined. A single crevice now ran along one side of the trunk, around the end, and back along the other side. She began to hear tiny splitting sounds, and the crevice gradually widened.

She pounded ever larger pieces of wood into the opening. In places, it was now wide enough for her to insert a hand, though she was careful not to do so. The groanings and gnashings from deep within the log sounded like the awakening of a powerful beast.

She concentrated her effort on the side of the log facing outward; here, the opening was widest, and before long there was room for the end of a pole. She used this as a lever and heaved her weight upon it.

There came a sound like the snapping of a great bone; the top of the log lifted for a moment. She repositioned the lever and leaned on it again. The sound was repeated, and some of the wedges fell out.

It was like opening an ancient sarcophagus.

The heavy lid protested all the way. Great daggers of wood appeared inside, snapping back into place as they broke. At last, the upper portion separated. She tilted the lid on edge and let it fall to the side. The interior of the log lay open to the sky.

From the number of ridges in the grain, she knew the tree had been growing when George III was king. Now it would bring about the salvation of a young woman born in the reign of Elizabeth II.

Already the log resembled a boat. The ends were blunt and blackened with fire, but the flat top and rounded sides still gave a strong hint of what was to come.

She immediately began to work down the outer contour into the sleek, double-ended shape that would give the hull speed as well as the ability to rise to the swell. She had decided to give both the bow and the stern a good amount of flare above the waterline, like the bow of a fast ship. Day by day, the charring of her fires ate away at the log. She became adept at using a piece of shell, probing to bare wood through the charcoal to monitor the progress being made. With several fires going at once, she was as much on the move as a chef tending a kitchen. The shifting wind made endless trouble. She had to channel errant flames with water-soaked balks of wood. Then again, the surface of the developing hull could be moistened to retard burning. In extreme cases, a coating of wet clay could be applied. Thus, adjacent areas could be exposed to the heat without risking those already brought to contour.

She lost track of the days, and it didn't matter. The new moon came, and this told her that it had been roughly three weeks since her arrival. Which was close enough. The status of missing and presumed lost carried with it one benefit at least — a person was not expected to keep appointments.

There came a day when it was no longer necessary to keep several fires alight. Now only a single, extended fire burned on the inside of the hull, eating its way steadily downward into the log's core. This inner fire required much less tending than had the others. It was sheltered from the wind, its progress was gradual and easily controlled, and there was a greater margin of safety. Only the edges of the developing wales had to be protected with a coating of clay.

She now worked at giving the exterior a better finish, using the long narrow shell of a barnacle for a gouge. Although the charcoal separated easily, the wood beneath could only be shaved away a bit at a time. She spread umbrella leaves to catch the waste, and every so often she would sweep the pile of shavings together and feed them to the fire inside the hull. Several days were spent in this way: working beneath the flaring sections, fore and aft; smoothing the contours; cleaning the wood wherever it was scorched.

It was a placid occupation, and didn't keep the mind enslaved as had the former task of tending several fires at once. With barnacle shell in hand, she worked steadily, her thoughts on other matters.

It was not so difficult now — remembering. Over the last three weeks the terrible sense of emptiness had gradually eased. She had more distance, more objectivity. It was like watching a caravan through binoculars. The Elly-puppet bobbed along with the others, smiling at times and highly animated; at other times moving slowly, head down, alone. The Elly-puppet was defined in terms of her father. He in turn was defined by his discovery of oriental pottery in a wild and unlikely place.

These had been the important elements in her life for as long as she could remember. She was the daughter of Doctor Jason Bradbury. All else followed. If he needed an assistant to advance his work, that assistant would be his daughter. Who else?

As inevitable as the turning of a planet.

Academic training would not be necessary. The by-passing of half a decade of schooling would make it possible for her to be at his side that much sooner. *He* would provide the needed training. "I need more than competence, Elena. Remember that. The work requires *brilliance*." He had said it any number of times. "Make no mistake: I need you. No one else will do."

But was it really true?

She'd never seriously questioned it before. But then, she'd never observed from such a distance before, either. The path chosen for her *wasn't* inevitable. Not really. In fact, it was beginning to look very much like a mistake.

She didn't *like* the work. She didn't find it rewarding.

On the other hand, perhaps her father was right. Maybe he *did* need her. She could be mistaken about that. (And it was so easy to make a mistake. Remember the forest fire? The one that *almost* happened?)

The very thought of it made her wince, though not for long. Every so often, one was granted the chance to redeem an error. And such was the case here. There was an element of the sublime — the way a lifeless timber, acquired in disgrace, could be transformed into a creation of worth.

Her boat was beautiful. Outside, it was the color of cinnamon. It had lean, hollowed lines, a sharp stem, a graceful stern.

Every day, she tested its weight. It was a great satisfaction to her when, at long last, a sufficient amount of wood had been removed, both from within and without, for her to lift either end by herself, without the aid of a lever.

The hull produced a soft, resonant note when she set it down.

She worked inside it now. The fire had gone as far as was safe, and the remaining cedar had to be removed by hand. Hour by hour. Day by day.

The barnacle shell was at its most efficient when it cut across the grain. It bit out a small, oval shaving with the sound of a carrot being sliced. The strokes, taken athwartship with the rounded edge of the shell, created a wave pattern on the inside of the boat, as if the wood were attempting to echo in miniature the flowing, liquid contours that would soon glide by on the outside. As the days passed, the tiny, leaflike shavings of cedar collected by the tens of thousands.

On a morning when the sun had just made one of its rare appearances, her work was interrupted by a sneezing sound from the direction of the water. She scrambled out of the bow, shedding chips as she went, and stood listening, telling herself that the sound had been a product of her imagination.

It wasn't.

With heart-stopping suddenness, a dark object as tall as a man reared above the surface of the bay less than a hundred meters off. It knifed forward like a moving tower, as black and glistening as wet vinyl.

Other towers appeared.

She could see the white patch at the base, and knew them to be orca — killer whales! For a time she was concerned for the safety of the crab pot, for these immensely tall fins were passing to the right and left of her marker float. But the animals navigated safely past, the vapor of their breathing showing now and then in the sunshine, accompanied by an explosive *puff-huff* as they exhaled and took another breath. The daggerlike fins rose and fell, as many as half a dozen coming to the surface at a time. One was larger than the others — about the size of a door, but not as symmetrical. That would be the patriarch. The bull.

Heading seaward, the pod of whales traveled grandly out of sight. It was sad to see them go, but then, the visitation had also been a reminder of the danger awaiting her at sea. These magnificent beasts were not known as killers for nothing.

In the days that followed, she made her usual trips with the raft to check the crab pot, but she wasn't as casual about it as she had been. She found herself keeping a continuous watch upon the waters of the bay, both near and far.

Then came an afternoon when the trap came aboard with a prisoner. She saw the flash of orange inside the cage as it neared the surface, and couldn't suppress a whoop of triumph, for it was exactly the shade of a dungeness crab.

She should have known better.

The carapace of the dungeness crab is indeed a lovely, bright orange — but only after it has been cooked. While the crab is alive, the top of the shell is the color of the sea bed: a dull, purplish brown. The creature in the trap was nothing more than a giant starfish, with what appeared to be a million arms. She had to take the trap ashore and remove the bottom before the starfish could be coaxed into releasing its multitentacled grip on the bars. Since the bottom was now unlatched, she decided it was time to experiment with a different type of bait.

Instead of the crushed barnacles, she used the overripe corpse of a raven that had washed up on the beach. It was a revolting chore, and she was greatly relieved to get the trap under water again and to resume her work.

The boat was nearing completion now. Instead of the dark charring of the fire, the inside of the hull displayed waves of tooling marks, running downward from each gunwale and across the bottom. The hull was a uniform two fingers in thickness everywhere except at the ends. Here, she had been forced to hollow out the wood in a rounded bowl shape, for a series of drying cracks had opened up in the surface, raising the possibility that the boat might try to split apart unless she gave it greater strength. The bow and stern were thus quite solid. Far better, she reasoned, to accept the penalty of a few extra kilograms of wood than to find oneself at sea with a hull that was splitting apart at the ends like a seed pod.

The last thing to be shaped was the top of the gunwale. She lavished great care on it, using a scraper of glass to give a satiny finish. This portion of the hull would be constantly handled, and it had to be as smooth as the surface of a piece of furniture.

She was almost sorry when the carving of the hull was done. It was evening. She wanted to put the boat in the water immediately, to try it out. There were a few structural details to be looked after, naturally, but these wouldn't prevent her from learning how the vessel rode. She decided, however, that it would be better to save the launching for the morning.

She built up the fire before turning in, and lay watching

the flames from within the shelter. Out on the beach, the newly carved hull seemed almost alive in the flickering light.

The boat still didn't have a name.

She'd thought of calling it *Theseus* for a time, but Theseus was a classical name; it made one think of a racing yacht.

Her boat should have the kind of name a Neolithic builder would have chosen. A name from the world of rocks and waterfalls, of soughing branches and the cries of wild things.

But the choice of a name was the least of her worries, as it happened. She began to turn fitfully on her pallet of branches, wondering about the practical aspects of the project. So much could go wrong! The wood, she told herself, was going to swell from contact with the water. Couldn't this localized expansion tear the hull apart? What had the ancients used to seal their wooden galleys? Pitch? She had only a few scraps of it. A dozen kilos would be needed to coat the outside of the hull. An impossibility! And what about the boat's underwater profile? Had she carried the wetted area too far forward? Would the bow take over and veer to the side when the boat was paddled? Had she built an unmanageable freak, good only for traveling in circles?

So ran her thoughts during the night. She was still awake at first light, but with the coming of day her apprehensions began to fade. A brisk wind blew from the south, and once she was up and moving about she found herself in a greatly improved frame of mind. The morning routines were carried out in a businesslike manner and when breakfast was over, she faced the new problem with solid confidence.

Her concern was over the boat's lack of a thwart.

The evening before, this had not been a consideration, for the bay had been as quiet as a pond. The dugout would have suffered no stress had it been launched in such conditions. In the last few hours, however, the weather had changed. A strong southerly was kicking up waves half a meter high. Instead of a quiet paddle in still water, the boat would have a severe test the instant it was launched. In all conscience, she couldn't go ahead with it unless the hull was given the lateral stiffening of a thwart. The quick, lifting force of a wave hitting the bow would tend to spread the wales and put a sudden outward stress on the end grain of bow and stern.

The boat *must* have a thwart.

Fortunately, the procedure had long since been decided upon; she could set to work without delay. The seat had already been cut to length from a section of plank. All she had to do was chisel a pair of rectangular slots through the hull amidships, one to a side, each positioned an equal distance below the level of the rail. The chips of cedar began to fly. The chisel nail and the mallet root seemed almost to operate themselves, for she had become skilled in their use over the last few weeks. The task was complete in a little over twenty minutes, and it had been done accurately, too. The thwart slid into place through the openings as if the slots had been made with a machine.

Just as well, she thought. The wind was growing

stronger. If the bay became much more boisterous, the launching would have to be delayed. With dirty weather in the offing, it might be days before she'd have another chance to give the boat a trial.

It was a race against the weather.

The edges of the thwart were beveled at their ends to match the angled surfaces fore and aft inside the slots. Working with a quickness and accuracy she'd never known before, she fashioned wedges to fit. She drove these into place. The boat now had a seat that gripped the hull at each side almost as firmly as if it had been bolted in place. For now, the wedges wouldn't need fastenings themselves; that would only take more time. If they began to work loose, she decided, she'd simply drive them in with a few blows of the paddle. For the moment, the seat could do without a compression brace in the middle. She'd remember to support most of her weight, canoe fashion, on her knees.

The boat was ready.

Out in the water, whitecaps had appeared. It was rough, but not impossibly so. She would be staying close to the beach in any case.

One final thing: the fire was whipping back and forth inside its makeshift house of planks, coming perilously close to being snuffed out by the heavy gusts. She added fresh fuel and a bit of additional protection in the form of ballast for the sheltering planks, which were in danger of being blown away. The fire could tend itself now — at least over the next half hour. She all but ran back to the boat.

"You will shortly be given a name, my friend," she

panted, hoisting the bow around so it pointed toward the water. The paddle board was placed ahead of the thwart where it could be reached when needed.

A wave came in. She dragged the boat across the sand trying to intercept the wave, but didn't quite succeed. The boat met only the last of it, and the stern remained firmly grounded. She shifted her position away from the bow and moved amidships, holding the thwart with one hand, the port gunwale with the other. She waited for the next wave. It gathered itself together, ten meters out, growing higher. She held tightly to the side of the boat as it approached. "I christen thee . . . " the bow lifted to the incoming wave, "I christen thee . . . *Water Bird!*"

The wave made a hollow thump as it collided with the bow. Two wings of spray appeared, arching to right and left as the boat's flare channeled the force of the blow, throwing the spray safely to the side.

As the wave swept under, *Water Bird* came alive.

15

It took five seconds, starting from the time the bow settled and the wave began to travel aft. It was like mounting a bicycle: you lifted one leg over the rail, rested your knee on the bottom of the boat, shifted your weight smoothly inboard, one hand on each rail, keeping everything in balance.

Three seconds.

Then you lifted the other foot from the water and brought it inboard. That could be done in approximately one second. Making four.

The rest, she estimated later, must have taken no more than a second. Making a total of five.

It was in that final second that everything came unstuck. She was reaching forward to pick up the paddle when the bay rose up from the left and smacked her in the side of the face. She was under water, and sand filled her mouth. Something hard delivered a stunning blow to her right shoulder. There was the *thock* of wood against bone.

She pulled herself clear of the surf and stood up. The top of her scapula hurt, but it didn't seem to be broken. She was all right — except for being wet, and having to spit out the sand in her mouth.

Water Bird was wallowing broadside. A wave would sweep it toward the beach, heeling it over. The boat would drift with the rush of water — sometimes bottom up, sometimes floating on its side, but never, never the right way up. The instant it grounded it began to roll. It rolled in with the wave. Then it reversed itself and rolled back out again. Like a barrel with one flattened side, thumping against the sand.

She captured it, emptied it out, and pulled it a short distance up the beach. She went over to the ledge and was about to climb . . . when her limbs went weak. Holding on to the ledge, she started hearing little bursts of laughter, like a child playing machine gun. Then it sounded more like an animal, so she made it stop. There was a bitter aftertaste from the sea water; what she needed was fresh water to wash it away.

She went to the grotto and knelt in the moss at the side of the little pool. The drink of water was refreshing. Since she was already wet, she washed the salt from her hair as well.

It had started to rain. Large, heavy drops. The wind roared among the trees and the rain felt almost warm.

The fire was in a bad way when she returned. As she moved one of the planks to feed it a bit of fuel, the wind almost snuffed it out. Her fire certainly wasn't going to help in drying her clothing.

Inside the shelter, she took off her wet things and wrung as much of the water from them as she could before getting dressed again. She lay down, the dried ferns and spruce branches crunching against the rock. The framework of the shelter protested as the gusts hit it. Spots of daylight would appear as the edges of the leaves lifted and fluttered. The leaves had become dry and brittle. But, amazingly, the shelter still held out the rain.

It was nice to build something that worked!

She fought the tears . . . and won. It helped a bit, remembering the lesson of the vaulting pole.

"Face it, Bradbury," she said. "Your boat's a bloody failure. It's no more stable than a rolling barrel!"

Poor *Water Bird*. Beautiful, graceful *Water Bird*.

"Stop that!" she commanded. "Get sentimental and you'll *die* here!"

The first thing to do was to figure out *why* the thing had failed. Then she'd have a better chance of fixing it.

She listened to the storm. The waves were nearer now, larger. She could hear the familiar thumping of the hull rolling against the beach.

She retrieved the boat once again. This time she dragged it up to the high water mark and tucked it between Cooking Rock and the pinnacle, turning it bottom up to keep out the rain.

A cedar log with pointed ends.

Looking at it upside down like this, she could see the reason. On that first day, she'd rested the log on its keel blocks. And then she'd left it there. From then on, the evolving hull had always been upright. As a result, the contour amidships had been determined by the shape of the log!

Rounded.

Like a barrel.

What she should have done was carve the bottom of the hull first, making it *flat*. Then the boat would have been stable. It would have had chines, like the native canoes she'd seen at the museum.

No help for that now; the hull had been carved. So the question was: How do you keep an unstable hull from rolling over? Add ballast? In the form of stones? There were two ways: either put the stones inside the hull, or suspend them underneath. But that'd do no good, either way. When placed inside the hull, the stones would be too close to the center of buoyancy. Too many would be needed. With that much weight, the boat would sink instantly, if swamped by a wave. Nor could the ballast be attached below. Using Stone Age fastenings, there'd be far too much drag.

The same drawback applied to the use of logs, strapped along each side.

It'd be like putting to sea on a raft.

Truth be told, her options were limited. It might be necessary to start afresh — do it all again.

The storm steadily worsened throughout the day. She was hard put to keep the fire alive, and the wind grew to such force that the wall of the shelter began to shudder violently. Working from inside, she applied dabs of warm pitch in an effort to glue down the wildly fluttering edges of the umbrella leaves. Even so, a number of them tore away. She blocked the openings with wads of fern from her bedding.

Sometime in the afternoon, there was a crash outside. The wind had knocked over the planks around the fire. She leapt instantly to save what she could, and it was touch and go for a while. She succeeded in rescuing enough of the coals to rebuild her fire inside the mouth of the shelter. She pushed her bedding back to make more room, and soon had a reassuring blaze going. With the protection of both the shelter and the planking, the fire behaved more normally. The smoke was not a problem, for the air inside the shelter was constantly changing. She lay with her feet before the flames and for the first time in hours enjoyed a degree of comfort. She might have a dry night after all.

Toward evening, she made a new foray into the maelstrom outside. *Water Bird* was in trouble again. The tide had risen much higher than usual, and her boat was battering itself against the driftwood. The surface of the bay seethed with whitecaps.

She turned the boat right side up, and hoisted the bow into the entrance to the tunnel. She stood on the ledge, pulling on the starboard rail. Every time a fresh wave pounded through the gap separating Cooking Rock from the pinnacle, she was able to hitch the hull a little higher. At last the boat rose onto the ledge with the sound of cedar grating against stone.

So concentrated was she upon the boat that she never saw the initial blow. There was a ponderous thump. She felt the shock of it traveling through the rock under her feet. Like an underground explosion.

A moment later, the shelter disintegrated, the pieces leaping up and scattering to the side as a white mass of water jostled its way along the ledge. The effect was precisely that of someone pushing a flat-bladed shovel along a snowy sidewalk. The moving shovel swept up everything in its path. Small pieces of what had been her home whirled about inside. She saw no more than this, for a second explosion claimed her attention. A fountain of spray leapt up on the other side of Cooking Rock, reaching forward like a clawed hand.

The wave pounded the boat from the ledge, and she went with it. There was a time of confusion and noise, and then the roaring quieted. Everything streamed foam. *Water Bird* was wedged between the rock and the pinnacle, lying on its side. She had one arm hooked around the thwart. The wave had turned and was rushing out, trying to take her with it. She held on. There was a hammering against the lower side of the boat. Charcoal, spruce branches, umbrella leaves — all went hurrying past.

As suddenly as it had come, the water was gone.

She stood up, but the sand yielded underfoot and she lost her balance and sat down. The water returned and carried her inside the hull. The force of the wave filled the boat and set it upright. Then the water went away again and left her lying inside the boat, like a bather in a tub.

She climbed out in time to meet the next one as it arrived. These were ordinary waves, she saw. They would do her no harm if she kept her wits about her.

The shelter was lost. She was going to need another.

Water Bird might lack the qualities of a boat, but it would make a good enough substitute for the destroyed shelter — if she could only get it to dry land.

She emptied out the boat. Once more she lifted the bow onto the ledge, this time from underneath. Another wave was coming. She went aft, picked up the stern and rested it on her shoulder while the water swirled around her legs. Carrying the stern around, she tossed it onto the ledge, climbed up herself, went forward, hopped out in front, tucked the boat's nose under her arm, and walked down the tunnel with it.

Submissively, *Water Bird* trundled along behind.

They didn't quite make it on their own. There was another explosion and the two of them were ejected out the landward end of the tunnel.

Water Bird dropped its nose among the umbrella leaves; she herself went sprawling in the mud. The ledge dribbled foam for a while. She was amazed at the amount of noise it made . . . until she noticed that the noise was coming from the tunnel as it collapsed.

The driftwood mountain had begun to heave itself upward, as if a dinosaur had crawled underneath.

She took *Water Bird* across the marsh to the bluff and stood it on its end. The bow rested among the trees at the edge of the bluff. In a breath, it seemed, she was on top, pulling the boat to safety in the forest.

In an unexpected spirit of helpfulness, *Water Bird* had become much lighter and easier to handle.

16

So *this* was the way the cove and the sandy beach had been created! Storms — from the southwest!

The great seas rolled into the bay, focused on the pinnacle as if by a titanic lens. High tide came several hours after the onslaught began, just as the sky was growing dark, and the effect on the Devil's acre of driftwood at the top of the beach was awesome. Entire trees rose from where they lay half buried in the sand and began to spin and leap.

She watched from the forest as the water created new landscapes below. Driftwood islands and promontories emerged as each wave retreated. Then all would be erased as the water returned, the entire mass churning to a thunderous, doomsday music. At one point, her former camp was buried under a wooden mountain. Seconds later, there wasn't a log within twenty meters of the place; as the tidal rush subsided, a great chasm opened up between Cooking Rock and the ledge.

She would have stayed at her post until dark, but the

bulwark of driftwood directly below chose to move elsewhere, leaving the foot of the bluff exposed. From the
yellowish color of the surf, she suspected that the marl
was being undercut, and decided to retreat up the mountain. Not long after, that section of bluff simply vanished,
removing a wide strip of forest. She didn't even hear it
go amid the general uproar, and was surprised when the
light around her suddenly brightened.

She spent the night under the overturned boat. For a
time, she slept.

By first light, an unnerving quiet had descended. She
stood in the rain at the lip of the newly formed cliff. The
tide was on the ebb, and it was this that gave the surf
its hushed, stealthy quality. The swells were still powerful, but they no longer reached the driftwood. Except
for an occasional thump as a wave hit the end of the
pinnacle, it was like watching television with the sound
turned off.

The beach below was hideous with yellow mud. The
remnants of the collapsed bluff formed a wasteland of
denuded roots, boulders, shattered trees. Sad little rolls
of spindrift wandered here and there across the wreckage.

Amazingly, the cove of the umbrella leaves was un-
touched. The mass of driftwood at the entrance had
defended the marsh against all intrusion. She went down
to the grotto for a drink of water and afterward returned
to the boat. The rain was unremitting. She passed the
time by watching a group of lethargic ants. With her
thumbnail, she made patterns in the soft wood of the
boat. She caught rainwater in her hand as it trickled off
the edge of the hull. The water tasted of cedar.

It was almost more than she could bear . . . to think of the plans she had made.

During the weeks of work upon the boat she had come to think of her time here as a summary — a shortened version of all that had happened over the last seventeen years. It gave things a feeling of balance, of design. As a child, her work had been to fashion herself into an adult; here in this wild place the work had been to build a boat. The boat was to bring escape from the place of its building. It had opened a door. And she'd been ready to step through the door into the world beyond.

And now the door had closed.

Throughout the second night and well into the following day it rained.

She ate the ants, and threw them up.

Then the rain ended. She found a route down the bluff in a place well beyond the pile of wreckage, for she had no desire to cross over from the marsh. The masses of driftwood hadn't had time to settle, and an avalanche of timber might be triggered at a touch.

The beach was a changed world. Between the hill of yellow rubble and the pinnacle there wasn't one recognizable feature. Logs the size of small houses now lay where once there had been open beach. Where the driftwood mountain had stood was now an enclosed valley, floored with sand. Even Cooking Rock was different. The sand had been stripped away from its base, making it higher. Wedged between it and the pinnacle — looking like a ship in dry dock — lay an enormous log. At its outer end was a pool of sea water. Shoreward, the log rested on the sand, and the water from the spring trickled along its outer flank.

Her shelter had vanished utterly. Only a brown smudge marked the place where the fire had been. Farther out, a few tattered ribbons of cedar bark still clung to the face of the cliff, but the larder and its precious supply of food were gone. All her possessions were gone: Bashing Tool, the fire tulip, the raft, the pieces of glass, her chisel nail, the mallet root, the aluminum cup, the plastic bottle. Even the crab pot was lost to her, for there was now no friendly bobber marking its location.

For an hour or more, she wandered the alien passageways of sand — slow-moving, hesitant, her eyes hungering for something that was not strange. When at last she spotted a branch that curved in a special way, it was as if the branch called out, asking to be plucked from its resting place. It lay at the base of a top-heavy mound of timber, but she ignored the danger and knelt in the sand below to rescue the branch from its shallow grave. She dug into the sand, her heart beating faster as she went. More and more of the branch appeared. When she reached the end of it, the strength of her emotion was such that it made a pain in her throat.

She had found her fire tulip — bent and crumpled, but intact. All twelve of the metal triangles were there.

Damaged though it was, the device was reparable.

What a magnificent piece of luck! She would begin again. She would build a new shelter. When the sun came out, she would kindle a fire. And with the fire would come all that made life bearable. Even escape was within her grasp once more, thanks to these few shreds of metal on the end of a stick.

There were many planks lying about. As a first step, she gathered them together and, for lack of a better place, stacked them on the ledge. She was going to have to decide where to locate the new campsite — perhaps on the other side of the pinnacle, she thought: above the beach of the stone soldiers — though without the plastic bottle, transporting fresh water would be a problem. She certainly didn't want to rebuild along the ledge; the very idea gave her goose flesh. Still, she didn't want to be too far from the clam beds, which would be accessible in another day or so, once the neaps were past. It *was* a problem. In the end, she chose to defer the decision until after she made a trip to the west. She was utterly famished, and the only chance of finding something to eat would be among the berry bushes along the bluff. It had been over a week since she'd gone to the west, and some of the fruit might now have ripened. There would also be salvage, left by the storm.

Looking back on it afterward, she thought there might have been an element of foreknowledge — as if she'd known what she would find, down past the wreckage of the bluff. Of course, this might have been an illusion. But there was still a *quality* about that journey: a feeling of remembering in advance.

She found several nails, embedded in wood rotten enough for her to remove the metal with her fingers. After that, she found a cardboard coffee cup, looking as fresh and white as if it had just come from the dispenser box. Tossed overboard from a ship, no doubt.

Ahead, a flash of yellow caught her eye. As she came nearer, she saw loops of cord projecting from the gravel. It was plastic — polypropylene, she thought — about as thick as that used with a Venetian blind, but instead of being braided, it was twisted, rope fashion, from three separate strands. It had lain a long time, protected by a covering of gravel. She must have walked over it several times in the past without knowing it was there. Now the storm had uncovered the cord for her, a piece of luck second only to finding the fire tulip.

As she pulled on the cord, it lifted from the gravel. She made a coil of it as she followed the trail up the beach. It ran under a piece of root, and was caught somewhere on the other side. She tugged. And the cord yielded. It was like one of those puzzle drawings where you're supposed to figure out how a set of pulleys and levers will work to produce the desired result.

Should you pull on the rope, or release it?

Will the axe hit, or won't it?

Which way should you jump? To the right or left?

The first log was the largest. And the slowest. She jumped over as it rolled by. Even as she did, she spotted the second one. It presented another problem altogether. Instead of rolling, the second log swung sideways through the air as it pivoted from somewhere within the grinding mass of timber above. No jumping. No ducking underneath. She threw herself to the left, but the cord snagged her foot and sent her sprawling. The leap to the side saved her, nonetheless. The end of the log swept harmlessly by and came to a stop, pointing toward the water.

There was a certain amount of shifting up above, but

the wooden machine was beginning to run down. Only a few secondary levers and counterweights slipped and bumped against one another. Down below, log number one had reached the water and was ponderously wading out into the bay.

"A bit too close for comfort!" she breathed, raising herself on one elbow.

Overhead, there was a scraping sound.

She glanced up in time to see the wooden machine spit out a narrow, crooked pole. The pole came arrowing down from the right. Slamming end-on against her ankle, it drove her right foot sideways into the gravel.

She was mostly astonished, for it didn't hurt much.

Then she moved to take a look and the pain that hit her, just above the joint, made her double over. It was a black-and-white movie — a gangster movie — where the police car, with its siren howling, comes tearing up to the curb. It was such a loud siren that it took her a moment to realize that she made the sound herself.

17

There were times when it hurt a great deal to move, and other times when it hurt less; the level of pain corresponded to the size of the stones.

Larger stones, more pain.

She tried standing with the help of a stick, but everything darkened and the beach whirled up and hit her in the face. After that she kept to the ground. For a while she moved inside a cloud made up of millions of hard little fleas. They got in her mouth when she breathed. Then she was past that place and there were no more fleas. She was glad to reach the sand, for the wrapped end of her leg didn't jar as much when sliding on sand.

Without thinking, she had headed for home . . . forgetting that she had no home. No shelter. No fire. Only the crumpled fire tulip and the log, wedged between Cooking Rock and the ledge. She pulled herself on top of the log and lay down, hoping the pain would let up, now that she wasn't moving. But it only grew worse. When it got to the point where she began to cry out, it occurred to her that the ankle might be swelling, creating pressure against the binding of yellow cord she'd used in an attempt to keep it immobilized.

She took off the heavy winding of cord. This helped somewhat. Evidently she had used too much tension. The pressure of dozens of overlapping loops would have been painful even without an injury.

It cost much effort and gritting of teeth to remove her shoe. When she finally got the stocking rolled down there wasn't much to see. A set of bruises had formed on the inside of the ankle, where the foot had been driven against the gravel, but the place where the blow had been struck — just above the end of the fibula — seemed hardly damaged. Pressing gently along the side of the bone, she thought she felt a slight notch.

She replaced the stocking, but not the shoe. Then she wrapped a pad of kelp leaves around her foot and ankle, and lightly wound on several layers of yellow cord.

Night came, and with it a bitter wind. In the dark, she found the lengths of plank on the ledge and used them to create a windbreak. She lay between the curving side of the log and the pinnacle, the planks resting on top. At high tide, the water came very close. She could hear the waves chuckling underneath.

The morning that followed was gray and windless. She looked into the sky and tried to smooth her mind into a mirror of what lay above. She could make the throbbing go away, but that was all. The person remained. There was no escape.

Before the arrival of the second night, she made a painful trip along the beach to the hill of mud lying beneath the newly formed cliff. Laboriously, she collected cedar branches from the wreckage. She unwound enough of the yellow cord to tie the branches into a bundle, and then dragged the bundle back to the log to create a pad for herself in the angle between the log and the rock. The planks were arranged to form a lean-to above, and that night she slept without their weight on her. After that she lost track. It might have been the third day, or the fourth, that she noticed the uncovering of the clam bed at low tide. She went down and dug until her hands could stand no more of the cold water. There were five clams. On breaking one of them open, she suddenly lost all desire to eat and threw it away, along with the others. Once a person was used to being without food, she'd discovered, it didn't hurt as much.

She did have water. She kept it in her paper cup. That way she only had to go to the end of the log once each day to drink at the stream. Besides the cup, the jacket pocket yielded up the nails she'd found. With one of these, she scratched a miniature checkerboard into the surface of the log. She made playing pieces of bark, and her days became a trifle less burdensome. Playing from the side of the board, she pitted her right hand against the left. Nearly always the right hand won, unless she gave a handicap.

On a gray evening no different from any of the others, she fell asleep over the board. When she awoke it was night, and yet brighter than before. The clouds had gone and a full moon turned everything to silver. The cold brilliance lighted up even the scratches of the checkerboard. She had raised herself on her elbow and was about to turn her head — for it had occurred to her that the beach must be lovely in the moonlight — when a sensation of terror descended and kept her from moving.

There was something, or someone, standing on the beach behind her. Although there was no sound but the lapping of the waves, she didn't doubt this conviction in the least.

She waited a long time. Instead of reassuring her, the stillness only made her more afraid. Then the silence was shattered by a sound very much like the venting of steam. An explosive *chuff*. A sound laden with violence and power, like that of a locomotive. She knew what it was, for she'd heard it only a month before. Up on the mountain.

She thought of escaping along the log to the shelter of the pool. But she knew the injury would slow her down. She wouldn't make it. And even if she did, the water was only a meter deep. She would be hunted like a fish in a stream, and the end would come quickly, down among the shadows under the log.

Her only chance was to remain still. And so she lay as rigid as a statue.

After the initial snort, there was silence. The sand muffled whatever footfalls there were, and it was left to one of her other senses to detect the animal's approach: her sense of smell.

There was a rank, musky tang. The hairs along her neck began to rise, for the odor had become overpowering. He was very close.

But instead of glimpsing him out of the corner of her eye, she saw the motion on top of the log immediately in front of her. A portion of her own shadow had begun to change. The intruding area of darkness was less substantial. The edge was blurred, indicating that the shadow was cast from a great height. The possibility crossed her mind that the creature might be standing on his hind legs.

Silently, the shadow stopped growing. It was still for a time, and then it began to move again, sliding along the outline of her shoulder, becoming smaller and more distinct as it dropped toward her elbow. It paused, reversed direction, and moved back. She watched the shadow the way a bird watches a snake. She was dying for air . . . but didn't breathe.

Again it stopped. Very slowly, the shadow began to merge with her own until the two were one. Feeling his closeness to the back of her neck, she waited. There was a soft but distinct *swishing* sound, as if a human had exhaled through the nose. This was repeated several times, and then there was complete silence.

She watched the edge of darkness on the surface before her, and was as still as her laboring heart would permit. Minutes passed, and still no sound. A long time went by. Slowly, her shadow lengthened as the moon swung across the sky.

And then she opened her eyes and it was no longer night. The morning sun lighted the mountains. The bay was a brilliant blue to match the sky, and it took a moment for her to adjust to the abrupt change: from a time of shadow and terror . . . to a morning both serene and warm.

Warily, she turned and eyed the beach. She was alone, except for the marks in the sand.

The footprints were huge.

But they weren't the footprints of a bear.

Instead of being square-shaped, with pads spreading to the side and long claw marks at the front, these prints were narrow, sharp-edged, deep. They had been made by the hooves of a buck.

She felt a surge of anger. She had been terrified of a *deer!* An animal so shy he would've bolted at the snap of a finger! She'd nearly died of fright, and to top it off, the creature had left a string of droppings across her beach!

Furiously, she snatched up a plank from the lean-to, used it as a crutch, and went hobbling out into the beach to bury every dark pellet she could find. She was out of breath when she got back. The yellow cord had come unwound from her foot. She stood on her good leg, leaning against the log and staring at the cord. It was the first time she'd actually seen it for what it was, and she grew angry all over again, this time with herself. The longer she looked at the cord, the more furious she became. If her right foot hadn't been broken, she would have stamped it. She had to be content with hitting the log with her fist.

"Dummy, dummy, *dummy!*"

She had a *cord!* She could have built a fire days ago! It was enough to make one weep with fury. She wasn't even certain how many days had been wasted — hadn't bothered to keep track — busy playing a *game!*

Like those women with their cards! Sitting *mummified* in their plane!

Lashing out with her arm, she swept the pieces from the board. From that moment she became a new woman. By the end of the day, a fire burned on the ledge. She had dragged a large stock of firewood across the sand, breaking the pieces to manageable size by smashing them against the rock. At low tide, she'd dug enough clams to fill the jacket, and then had towed it back to camp. After that, she'd steamed and smoked the clams. She'd used the yellow cord as a climbing rope and had scaled the bluff to dig sword ferns in the forest. The roots were broiled in the fire. By evening, she had eaten a number of small meals, a bit more each time. The leftover food she stored away. She had made a replacement for the vanished larder of vines, this time using her bra. The bra was fastened by the straps at the top of a pole. She wedged the pole upright between the log and the pinnacle, so that the new larder hung high in the air where no animal could reach.

In the course of that day, she'd evolved a new creed: Pain was to be treated with contempt. The injured foot might slow her down, but it would not stop her. Nothing would stop her. If a thing needed doing, then it would be done, pain or not. The game — the *real* game — had yet to be played out. She had several months before the cold weather: several months to live. If she were to go down, it would be with one hell of a fight!

The *creed* had become a part of her. It colored every action, every thought, and went so far as to invade her dreams. She found herself in the tropics, surrounded by a joyous throng. She was on an island where fires lit the night. The people danced to the throbbing of drums, and as she listened she felt a passionate desire to join in the dance. Cries of alarm rang out as she struggled to her feet. Dissuading hands reached toward her, and a wave of pain rolled upward. "I will overcome it," she told them. "I will dance." And the pain receded. Lo! She was dancing! Spinning round and round in the firelight. She could see the gleam of eyes and the flutter of many hands. To the beach she went, among the hundreds of native craft: surfboards, canoes, trimarans, outriggers. She whirled among them like a ballerina, supported not by faltering, pain-ridden feet, but by determination.

Unyielding. Unstoppable.

She woke to a gray and rainy morning. But in her mind the fires still winked and flickered, and the boats along the beach seemed almost as alive. Despite the rain, she felt a sense of exhilaration, of triumph. For the dream had been a gift. It provided the solution.

The key!

To the prison door.

18

She chiseled a hole into the stem, making two openings right where the hawse holes would be on an ocean liner. She'd taken the yellow cord from her foot, replacing it with a binding of cedar bark, and so was able to reeve the end of the cord through the hole to create a twofold purchase. The boat was under firm control all the way down to the edge of the cliff. From there, it was touch and go. The vessel dangled against the face of the bluff like a hooked fish, and the reach of her tackle was insufficient for lowering it the rest of the way to the beach. In desperation, she improvised a braking device of half hitches and let go the running part of the line. When the dust cleared, *Water Bird* rested unhurt atop the ocher-tinged rubble, its bow pointed toward the water as if it were eager to be off and swimming in its natural element.

She heaved a vast sigh, for had she miscalculated, the boat would have shattered like a dropped piano on the rocks.

It was a greatly altered *Water Bird* that lay beside Cooking Rock forty-eight hours later. Two long spruce limbs lay across the gunwales, one forward, one aft, each projecting over a fathom's length to port. A natural curve in each of the branches caused their ends to dip downward, and the tips were wedged into holes bored through a balk of driftwood fifteen centimeters thick. *Water Bird* was now an outrigger. The balk of timber was the float, lying level with the waterline and parallel with the hull. The whole affair was extremely sturdy. The projecting poles were fastened to the top of the rail with heavy lashings of cord, stitched directly into the sides of the boat. Even laden with rocks, the vessel could have been lifted by the poles alone, so stoutly were they held in place.

Levering her crutch against the forward outrigger pole, she moved the boat down to the water. Although the bay was calm, she had left her shoes, stockings, and trousers back at camp. She was taking nothing for granted this time; if she ran into trouble there'd be only a set of panties and a wool shirt to wring out — the ever-present signal mirror around her neck could take care of itself. As a gesture to safety, she had tucked the flotation jacket under the seat.

Water Bird slid quietly into the water, riding the surface like a great wooden swan with one wing extended. She hopped one-legged through the water and sat on the port rail amidships. It was a severe test — one a rowboat would not have passed. *Water Bird*, however, took it all in stride; there was only a moderate dipping of the float.

So far, so good.

Feeling a twinge of unease, she gingerly climbed aboard. She needn't have worried; the boat was now amazingly steady.

She put a hand on each rail and rocked violently from side to side . . . almost no bending of the poles. The spruce-limb outrigger might as well have been made of steel pipe.

Reaching forward, she picked up the paddle she had made and took her first stroke with it. Nothing much happened. It was a tentative stroke and *Water Bird* had considerable inertia.

She took half a dozen more, and was astonished at the speed that developed. The boat, she estimated, was up to two and a half knots, and when she stopped paddling it kept right on going. Thirty seconds later, *Water Bird* was still making a knot and a half, gliding effortlessly along as if it would never stop. She took a dozen powerful strokes and worked up to a speed of well over three knots. At this velocity, however, a great deal of energy was needed, and once she stopped working, the speed dropped off rapidly until it was down to an estimated two knots. This was the point where the chuckle of the water died away and the boat began to move silently, slowing only gradually and creating little wake.

Slight changes in course, she found, could be made by shifting one's weight.

So engrossed had she become in her observations that she almost ran the boat aground. For a moment she couldn't imagine where she was, for the beach ahead was unfamiliar. With a growing sense of panic, she looked around for the pinnacle . . . and couldn't find it. It was like dropping off the edge of the earth. *Nothing* was familiar.

The explanation, when it came, was simple. Out of long habit, she had maintained a constant heading and had crossed the bay! There on the opposite shore was the pinnacle, dwarfed by the expanse of mountain above.

She was filled with delight at the ease of the journey. *Water Bird*, she decided, was like a magic carpet. With the first stroke of the paddle, her freedom of movement had been multiplied a thousandfold.

It was a miracle too large to be taken in at once.

Turning westward, she paddled along the strange beach until she came to a place where *Water Bird* began to swoop and plunge. Breakers roared against the beach to port. On the other side of the entrance was the patch of shingle where she had left the raft — long ago it seemed. A chill wind came down the strait from the northwest, forcing her to don the jacket, but she maintained her course, fighting a stiff current, for the tide was on the rise. Past the shelter of the northern rocks she came to open water and was concerned at first over the abrupt motions the boat made when the chop was abeam. This, however, was only the product of a high stability. *Water Bird* was merely following the contours of the sea.

She altered course to windward, driving the boat as swiftly as she could into the swell. It was the final and most arduous test. *Water Bird* pounded against the water, throwing curtains of spray to the side after each lunge from the top of a wave. The shock would set the outrigger vibrating like a tuning fork, but there was no sign of damage.

After an hour of learning *Water Bird*'s ways in rough water, she headed back, allowing the great river of the tide to carry her north and east into the bay. The boat glided effortlessly along the well-remembered stretch of beach: past the wooden machine, crouching evilly below the bluff; past the long stretch of shingle that had cost such an eternity of pain the last time she'd come that way. As she neared the pinnacle, she chanced to look down, and saw something dark slide by. She turned the boat and went back, going more slowly this time.

It was the up-haul branch, minus the bobber but standing watch as before under the water. She pulled it up and discovered that the trap was still attached. In place of the dead raven there were now two dungeness crabs — very much alive, and scrabbling frantically inside the cage.

She dined well that evening, as did the raccoons, who made their appearance as soon as the smell of cooked crab went out on the breeze. She fed the raccoons the white breather sacks, which she didn't want, and scolded them roundly for being fair-weather friends. Scipio Africanus and Company tussled over the handouts, and she laughed at the sight. It was a marvelous feeling. She was in control. For the very first time, she knew herself to be an adult, capable of making her own decisions.

Capable.

She had never looked at herself that way before. Neither had anyone else — except for Pauline. After all, wasn't it Pauline who kept hinting at "old Elly's" hidden talents? "You're never given credit for the things you're *really* good at, chum," she'd said one time.

And her friend was right.

She understood any number of things that mystified her father. In a way, it was funny. "They're sending an inferior grade of electricity through the wires this morning," he'd mutter, querulously. And this would tell her that his electric razor had begun to bog down and that it was time for her to take the cutter head apart, clean it in solvent, and give it a little oil in the right places. She always did this secretly, for fear of her aunt's displeasure. Over breakfast the next morning, her father would comment that the electric utility was "shipping the genuine article" along to them once more, and then, like as not, there would come the usual discussion about the scheduling of Dear Elena's transport for the day . . . it being understood that Dear Elena could never be allowed to drive the automobile herself because she lacked the necessary *mechanical* insight!

She'd been a closet mechanic all her life!

There were other things too. She was good at charts, diagrams, blueprints — anything practical — which was fortunate. Here inside the bay a person was either practical or dead!

And she liked designing things.

There was a name for that. She wouldn't have dreamt of associating the discipline with herself before, but it was the obvious linkage — now that *Water Bird* had grown from an ugly duckling into a quick and stable swan.

What do you call someone who designs things: who

calculates stresses, angles, contours, volumes, toler-
ances?

Engineer.

You call such a person an engineer.

As she went to sleep that night, it was with the knowledge that she had built far more than a boat. *Water Bird*
was part of something larger. The *something* was still vague,
but it was so close . . . she could almost touch it.

19

There was no feeling of sadness at leaving. Three days had passed since the launching. During this time the weather had been foul, and she'd waited with impatience for the coming of good visibility and a moderate wind. On the morning of the fourth day the air was calm, but there was a heavy fog. It was almost noon before the fog burned off. The sound of the surf outside the entrance now indicated the arrival of a fair-weather wind from the northwest. Time to go.

Her possessions, secured for sea inside the boat, were few. The fire tulip, her store of food, her crutch, a spare paddle, a scrap of yellow cord, and her right shoe, which would function as a bailer, should one be needed. The crab pot had served its function and was left on the ledge beside the dead fire. She drank deeply at the spring, knowing it would be the last fresh water she would see for some time. After leaving a final present of food for the raccoons, she pushed off.

She did not look back. Her camp at the base of the

pinnacle was not what it had been before the storm. The waves had erased all that she had valued. The sandy beach had changed. It was no longer the birthing ground of *Water Bird*. That place was gone. The thing that remained could offer her only a lingering death.

Outside the bay, the wind was cold. It drove a moderate sea before it, and *Water Bird* twisted and plunged, taking the swells on the starboard bow. She paddled steadily to the west. Her plan was to put a nautical mile or so between herself and the cliffs before deciding on the precise course northward. She wanted to have as complete an understanding of the coastline as possible before committing herself. Spray came aboard, and she was grateful for this. Already, she was becoming a trifle seasick. The shock of the cold water against her face helped greatly in combatting nausea.

Looking back she saw that the entrance was at least a mile behind her now. But it didn't seem far enough. She held her course to the west until she'd gone a mile and a half. Then two miles. Each time she looked back, the distance covered did not suit her. By now, she could see past the northern cliffs. There was a twenty-mile strait with an island on the other side. She recognized the shape of the island, even though the tall silhouette was blue with distance. It was Torroba. The island of her father's camp.

Not a place with a happy history, Torroba Island. A thousand years before, the survivors of a lost and desperate fleet had come there . . . and died.

She knew the island well. There was an inlet, leading between the mountains. At the end of the inlet there was a marsh. A dock. A collection of tents with netting at every opening, for the marsh swarmed with mosquitoes. And behind the tents were the rectangular holes, dug in the earth. Like graves.

Her arms were heavy. She could hardly lift them to make the stroke. After a time she gave it up, allowing *Water Bird* to drift. She released the paddle and rubbed the spray from her face. She couldn't remember feeling this way, ever before. It was like the churning of the driftwood during the storm. For a time, she could make no sense of it. And then a conviction formed in her mind. It was not a matter of logic. The thing was more compelling than that. She knew — she *knew* she could not go to the north. She could no more return to that mosquito bog at the end of the inlet than she could walk again beneath the pinnacle. The two places were the same.

They were the same!

And so it was settled. There was only one direction remaining.

With a feeling of relief, of having avoided a terrible error, she swung *Water Bird*'s bow to the southeast. Downwind. The boat glided forward without effort, and the rocky face of the island reeled past on the port side. The speed was exhilarating. New headlands and mountains appeared. For an hour she crossed the mouth of an open bay, and then she came to a place where tall sea stacks rose from the ocean. Hundreds of gulls whirled in the air above; the sea broke in sheets of spray at the waterline. Later in the afternoon the wind increased, as did the size of the waves. She was wasting her energy paddling. When a new reach of shoreline opened up, one with no obstructions, she raised the crutch as a foremast, and hoisted the jacket as a sail. The spare paddle acted as the yard, and she made the rigging with pieces of unraveled yarn from the yellow cord.

The day was brilliant. With *Water Bird* running before the wind, she lay flat on her back, her head cradled in the rounded bowl of the stern. The motion of the sea was not as unsettling for the stomach when one was lying down. She almost fell asleep, listening to the rhythmic swish of the water. The wind could not reach her, and the sun was warm.

Perhaps as many as twenty nautical miles slipped by before she came upon the first traces of civilization. The sun had swung around until it was almost behind her, low in the sky, and in the long, golden light, the side of a mountain showed brown against the sky. The forest had been stripped away.

She put in to shore and found a narrow cove, sheltered by a reef. At one side of a placid lagoon was a dock, and on the hillside above stood a gantrylike affair of timbers and a long shed of weathered planks. Down at the end of the lagoon rested the hulk of a dilapidated barge, half under water. There was little else. Going ashore, she found the shed to be completely bare. Above the dock there was a level place, floored with bark, while off in the weeds lay a rusty engine and a pile of cans and bottles. She judged from the refuse that the men who had felled the trees of the mountain had lived mostly on whiskey.

She salvaged a couple of the liquor bottles and went to look for water. She found nothing: no sign of either a spring or a well, not even a brackish puddle of rain water. Feeling that she had wasted her time, she headed southward again, taking the two bottles with her in the hope of encountering a spring.

As the light waned, the wind began to slacken. She took down her makeshift sail and paddled in the dusk, keeping an eye to port for a suitable place to land. With the dropping of the wind, the waves grew smaller and smaller, leaving only a swell from the south. The shore curved to the east here, and the mountains were little more than hills. It was growing too dark for her to see clearly, but it was evident that she was approaching the southern tip of the island.

On rounding a small headland, she had the distinct impression of seeing a light, just for a moment, out of the corner of her eye. There was an interval of several seconds during which she peered intently into the gloom, a couple of points forward of the port beam. Then the light came again: two very brief, but very distinct winks. A signal, coming from the end of the next point.

For a time, she dug her paddle into the water with a will, but only for a time. The blinks were repeated with mechanical regularity — two flashes, one second apart, followed by nine seconds of blackness. On and on. Mindlessly.

An aid to navigation. A robot.

She pulled out on a short, steep beach, and made her way up a crude path to the top of the point. The battery box was raised on a metal stand, and she used her arms and her one good leg to climb the ladder to the platform. The box was the size of a washing machine, painted white. On top was a small, heavily reinforced lantern. She could hear the grinding of the timer inside.

With her eyes still dazzled by the afterimage of the flashing light, she returned to the boat. The moon was in its last quarter, and by its radiance she could see a wide channel running to the north along the eastern side of the island. Far off were the running lights of a tug, pulling a barge. She was beside one of the arteries of the inland passage, an intricate network of sheltered, deep-water channels running from the cities of southern British Columbia all the way to Alaska. If she were to find help, it would be here.

Out of a sense of duty, she got out one of the leaf-wrapped packets of smoked clam meat, but then didn't eat it. The food would only make her more thirsty. She found a mass of dried seaweed and made a bed in the bottom of the boat. Even with her eyes closed, the blinking of the robot lighthouse kept intruding. She covered her eyes with her arm and tried to imagine the sequence of events . . . had she gone north that morning, instead of south.

A twenty-knot head wind.

She would have slaved at the paddle throughout the day, and by now her hands would've been raw meat.

And how far would she have gone?

Not far enough. She'd still be at sea — at the limit of her strength — paddling in the dark, and far more thirsty than she was now.

To be honest, however, that hadn't been a consideration at the time. Her choice had not been made on the basis of the journey's difficulty, but because of its destination. Seeking refuge at her father's camp would have been a form of acquiescence . . . to the path he had chosen for her.

His loyal servant.

His subordinate in a field for which she was not made.

No wonder she'd reacted as she had to the thought of going north! It was part of a new understanding of herself: the knowledge that she was now an adult. She had earned that status the hard way, and the time of passivity, of *going along* with whatever others might plan was over. Her father was a determined man, and would resist her decisions, but now she knew a thing or two herself about determination!

Deny her the chance to earn *credentials*, would he? Deny her schooling? And the right to choose a field?

Not bloody likely!

Doctor Jason Bradbury was about to have a little surprise. (Two, actually, if you counted the fact that his daughter was still alive.) Dear Elena had undergone something of a sea change, and was not the same timid creature who had stepped aboard the plane to Torroba six weeks before. She was not to be swayed. Dear Elena was going to control her own life. As she had every right to do.

Lying in the darkness, she felt a great anger, and for a time she fueled the anger. The list of oppressions was a long one. Adding it up, she saw that she had been granted but one freedom — to go on the water. And thank God for that! Her knowledge of the water, of boats, had been a major element in her survival. Without it, she would have gone the way of her mother, and at yet an earlier age.

My Beautiful Wife, ran the words of the stone. The dates gave a span of twenty-eight years. Always, that had seemed an enormously long time for a person to live. Not now. Twenty-eight was really quite young — a third of what might have been. She had never cried for her mother before, but she did so now, even though it was for a person she could not remember. And in the middle of her grief, she began to see the husband of that phantom personality in another light.

It was strange: how you could know a thing, and still *not* know it.

My Beautiful Wife.

He had never spoken of it, and now she saw that this was because of the pain. It must have followed him everywhere.

But still, there had been the daughter, maturing into the exact image of the one who had been lost. His beloved young wife, alive again. Reborn.

Could he really be blamed? For clinging so tightly?

20

It was a quiet morning of low clouds. Out to sea, a freighter moved along the horizon. In the other direction, the continent showed a dark, brooding face, marked with the scars of lumbering. From north and south came two vast channels, joining together at the opening between the islands. It was a major outlet to the sea. With the tide ebbing, the water slid against the eastern side of Gedney like the flow of a river, moving south. Whirlpools formed off the end of the point.

She was about to depart when she felt an overwhelming need to leave a mark on Gedney Island, a sign that she had come this way. Struggling up the path, she returned to the light and again climbed the metal ladder to the platform. With one of her salvaged nails, she scraped her name into the painted side of the battery box. Then she wrote the month, the year, and the notation: SUR-VIVED PLANE CRASH.

It didn't seem to be enough. Inscribing more lightly now, she gave the date of the crash, a description of the bay, the wreck's location, Jim's name, a brief history of what had followed — all in sentences of two or three words, as in a telegram.

Instead of printing, she carved her signature at the end. To show authenticity.

It had taken an hour, but it was with a much lighter heart that she descended to the boat. Pain had become an old acquaintance now; she didn't allow thirst or protesting muscles to slow her down. *Water Bird* glided as swiftly as before, this time to the east. It was her plan to cross to the mainland — or, to be more exact, to one of the long extensions of the mainland — on the other side of the channel. Several hours at a steady two and a half knots ought to do the trick. If she was lucky enough to intercept a passing boat or a tug on the way, then well and good. If not, her chances of finding fresh water and people would be better, cruising the edge of the larger land mass. It didn't matter to her which came first, the water or the people. If she found water, she would no longer be thirsty; if she found people, they would undoubtedly have water.

Water was the important thing. After an hour's labor at the paddle, her thirst had become impossible to ignore. Wistfully, she recalled the loss of the paper cup several days before. The thing had fallen apart; otherwise she would have made some sort of a top for it, and would have had at least a token amount of water to take with her on the voyage.

"Oh, *really* now!" she admonished herself. "It wouldn't have been that much of a help. The water would be long gone by now, and your throat would be every bit as dry."

Not long after, she heard the engine of a plane.

The craft had swept in from the south unnoticed — a small float plane, traveling fairly low and making little sound. It was crossing astern of her, less than a kilometer away. Instantly, she backwatered, whipping the boat broadside on. While *Water Bird* was still turning, she took off her jacket and waved it with such energy the boat made ripples in the water. She shouted also, even though she knew she couldn't be heard.

For a moment, it looked as if they hadn't seen her. And then she knew they had. Brightly, the way an engineer waves to a child beside the track, the plane rocked its wings and flew on.

She watched it go, unwilling to believe. She expected the thin line of the wings to tilt and widen — for the plane to bank into a turn and come back. But it didn't.

The plane grew smaller and smaller, heading up the strait to the north. By degrees, incredulity turned to rage. She had seen their faces! How could anyone, *anyone* ignore such vehemence? For a time, she could only curse them. But then her analytical nature asserted itself. Perhaps, she thought, they had seen her from a long way off. They might even have altered course for the purpose of greeting this active paddler in her obviously seaworthy craft. There would be no way of knowing that her ankle was broken: that she was in need of water. They would have expected her to *stand* had anything been wrong.

But the little figure in the outrigger had remained seated. Her posture had given a confused signal: partly passive, partly active. Because of this, the waving of the jacket would have seemed to them to be mere exuberance, not desperation.

She headed east once more, and the going was hard. Her hands were blistered now; the muscles of her upper body and arms felt lacerated and seeded with glass. The current was carrying her to the south. In the interest of conserving her strength, she didn't fight it and kept a course that was perpendicular to the coast. The ease of the crossing was what was important, not the point of landing.

By midmorning, her goal was only three or four kilometers away. A fast cabin cruiser went by, maneuvering in and out of the obstructions along the beach. Those aboard did not see the waving jacket; like the plane, the cruiser disappeared to the north.

The water had become glassy in places. Whenever she crossed the rip between one smooth patch and the next, *Water Bird* would give an odd little swerve to the side. It was an area of opposing currents. When it became evident that the land was coming no nearer, she upped the stroke rate from a leisurely twenty-four per minute to thirty. Shortly after that she increased the pace again: one stroke every one and a half seconds, ten strokes every fifteen seconds, forty strokes a minute. Forty vigorous strokes. She breathed like a runner, through her mouth. Minute by minute, the work became more brutal. But she was determined not to be carried away from the mainland. Slowly, *Water Bird* began to gain in this race for the shore. But the beach was still slipping past the bow. She crabbed into the current slightly to reduce the drift. It would be a very bad idea to allow the next point of land to slip by. On the other side would be the north-bound current, which would create a swift flow to sea-ward, as it rushed against the one she was riding.

She had wondered why the cruiser remained so close to shore. Now she knew.

There was a sound of fast water — a hushed, silken, tearing noise. To starboard, a great log came drifting on the polished surface. The log was like an ancient galley, trying to ram. But then it halted, a stone's throw away. It swiveled broadside, quivered, lifted half its length from the water, stood upright, and then it vanished. Straight down. Swallowed whole by a narrow crevice, marking the join between currents. *Water Bird* was car-ried sideways toward it. The paddle was useless. There was a shudder, a thump, as the hull dropped into the depression. *Water Bird* sped to the west, toward the open sea.

Exhausted, she lay down. "It's all right, *Water Bird*." She patted the gunwale. "We lost the race but at least we made it through the rip. If you'd had as rough a surface as the log, or had run out of luck, then the water would have pulled you under too, and neither of us would have come to the surface yet. Did *you* see the log come up? I know I didn't. Maybe it's still down there."

The land was departing. She was about to tell *Water Bird* that this would not be a problem, that they'd have another try when the tide changed . . . but she was feel-ing very shaky and weak. It would be best not to make any promises in that department. She felt a *moving* sensation now, as if an army of grubs were tunneling from within. It wasn't painful, only the thirst was painful. That long sprint had been far more draining than she would have expected, earlier. But then, there had been the six long weeks of privation, the thirty hours without water.

The machine had done all it could, poor thing.

"I'm sorry, machine," she said. "I should have known. There's a physical limit, isn't there? Determination can only do so much."

The hand on the rail was mostly bone. Bone and tendon, wrapped in skin. Much of the muscle and all of the fat had melted away. The machine was consuming itself. Poor, beautiful, lithe, resilient, self-repairing machine. Some of its blood had leaked out. Onto the handle of the paddle. Onto the rail.

"It's all right for *you*," she said. "You're made for it. It's your field. But it's got nothing to do with me. I don't *like* digging after other people's bones! I like *making* things!"

She could see the park where they used to take their walks. And the green-painted bench overlooking the marina. It had been there as long as she could remember, that bench. It was the place for serious talk.

"I need training," she would tell him. "The regular courses — for engineering — plus the ones for the specialty." She paused. Then she said the words slowly: "Marine architect." She savored the sound of it. "Maybe I'll go to the U.K. to finish up. I don't know. Have to look into it. But whatever it takes . . ."

She could see lines on paper. Wood and steel and

Fiberglas, rising on the stocks. Then the finished hulls. White. Gleaming. Slender or powerful, depending on the work for which each boat had been designed.

They would be her children. Her creations — graceful hulls, greeting the sea with proper ceremony.

The light had gradually become stronger. She could feel the heat of it on her arms and forehead. She smiled into the glare, knowing the sun to be her friend.

Bright sunlight. And her signal mirror.

So she'd been right to go south instead of north.

She'd been right.

Had something to live for now.

Epilogue

The chief engineer noticed it first.

"Hullo!" he said, "we're slowing down."

Captain Van de Velde, immaculate in fresh whites, his bulk nearly filling the passageway, turned and glared at the propeller shaft.

Sure enough, it rotated more slowly, and the thunder of the starboard screw had taken a leisurely beat. Without a word, the captain spun on his heel and strode off down the tunnel.

First an overheated bearing, he thought. Now this! If he hadn't been beached, he'd never have taken this flag-of-convenience bucket!

Emerging into the oily warmth of the engine room, he made for the after phone station, and was in the act of dialing when the engines thudded to a stop. There was a hiss of air, and then the diesels reversed, rumbling back to life. The ship was backing down. Full astern.

Slowly, he replaced the receiver. A call to the bridge at this point would only distract the watch, he decided.

No matter what was going on, intervention should be based on firsthand knowledge. Conning a liner from the shaft alley was for fools.

It was a long climb to the bridge, but Van de Velde covered the nine decks in record time. "Tried to get hold of you, sir . . ." began the quartermaster. The captain waved him off and continued his march to the starboard wing, where the second officer and the cadet were craning their necks overside.

"Got an S O S, Captain," said the second, looking up. "Small boat, sir. Flashing light. Somebody's injured, but Doc Ramirez is on the way." He raised his voice to reach inside the wheel house. *"All stop! Rudder 'midships!"*

Already, several hundred passengers crowded the rail of the promenade deck, all of them looking down. Following their example, Van de Velde saw that a door in the side of the ship, the one to the forward storeroom, had been latched open. Underneath lay a bizarre little craft, barely large enough for two people. A Jacob's ladder dangled inside the gunwale. The boat had nobody in it.

"That was quick!" grunted the captain.

"Used that paddle like a pro!" replied the second. "Pretty good with Morse, too."

Van de Velde was not as favorably impressed. His sailor's eye noted the lack of varnish, the outrigger poles with the bark still on them, and the empty liquor bottles.

The inland passage swarmed with such boats.

"Riffraff!" snorted the captain. "Have you set up One-Way Containment?"

"Yes, sir. Both entrances. Edwards on one, coxswain on the other. There's a steward holding the phone."

"Good." One-Way Containment was Van de Velde's innovation. Whenever the ship was boarded, no one could leave the affected compartment until One-Way Containment was lifted. The year before, a group of spaced-out idiots in a boat not much different from this one had decided to call an emergency, just for laughs. Niburg, on the *Freya*, had experienced hours of trouble once he let them aboard, and Van de Velde was determined that no such thing would occur on *his* command. With OWC now in effect, he could focus on a matter of more immediate concern — the preservation of a large ship in treacherous waters.

It had just been demonstrated that the liner was not about to go aground, when the quatermaster, his ear to the phone, passed on the information that the young lady had been struck on the foot by an airplane.

The captain scowled. "Struck on the foot by a *what?*"

"An airplane, sir. I *think* that's what he says. Allepo's English isn't too good." The man tried to hand him the receiver.

"Get hold of the doctor," demanded Van de Velde.

"It is not a serious injury, Captain," said Doctor Ramirez when he came on the line. "I will need the x-ray, naturally. But I suspect only a green twig bend. Very painful, yes. Dangerous? No. However, she needs treatment. Care. There is malnutrition. Dehydration. All together a very bad experience. We must take her with us."

"Fine," said Van de Velde. "May I speak to Mister Sawyer, please?" He was relieved to hear about the injury — that there actually *was* an injury. This obvious fiction about the airplane had sounded like a cover story designed to give these people access to the ship. For a moment there he had imagined the woman's accomplice — dirty, zonked-out, no doubt bearded — slipping past the guard, racing through the passageways on some insane errand of his own . . .

"Sawyer here, sir."

"Yes. Listen, Harold. This delay'll be costing us fuel in the morning — bucking a runout — so get that piece of *junk* cast off, will you? We're offering medical assistance and a free ride to the woman — the companion too, if he wants — but no more than that. Understood?"

"Well . . . I don't know if she'll go along with it, sir. Seems to me . . ."

"Beggars can't be choosers, Hal," snapped Van de Velde. "If anybody wants to reembark, I'll give 'em time to get clear. Otherwise cut the blasted thing loose. I don't give a damn if it's chopped up in the screw! So get on with it."

"Yes, sir."

The captain handed over the phone and went out on the starboard wing where he stood, hands behind him, controlling his impatience. When at sea, the ship's operating cost was measured in dollars per second. Having waited for precisely one minute, he crossed to the rail.

The boat was still there. A crew member's hat had fallen into the bow, and there was a flurry of motion at the open hatch as if a scuffle was taking place.

Van de Velde reentered the wheel house. *"Number two!"*

"Sir?"

"I'm going below. Give me four minutes." He looked at his watch. "If you don't hear from me by then, get us out of here. Same course. Wind 'em up to eighty turns!"

Let these people argue with the momentum of a twenty-thousand-ton ship! he thought, making his way below.

The storeroom, when he reached it, was a madhouse. A hundred people surged about the opening in the ship's side, everyone shouting at once, so that individual words were like pebbles, tossed into a roaring surf. Grim-faced, Van de Velde pushed onward.

A blanket of silence followed after him, and by the time he reached his goal, the tumult had subsided into a soft shuffling of feet; a sound of breathing.

"What's the problem here?" demanded the captain. Sawyer, the doctor, and a number of others were clustered about a slender scarecrow of a girl, standing in the open door. She was silhouetted against the glare from outside. It seemed to Van de Velde that there was something regal in her stance, despite her naked foot and her grasping of a latch handle for support. He dismissed the impression. There was nothing of value here. Her clothing was filthy and daubed with pitch. Every element of beauty had been sullied by willful neglect.

He knew her kind.

Sawyer was mumbling something about the boat. Irritated with such unprofessional behavior, Van de Velde cut him off: "Where's this *boy*friend?" he asked.

The response was even less professional than the mumbling had been. First Officer Sawyer opened his mouth, but no sound came out.

"*You,*" snapped the captain, turning to the ragged stork in the doorway. "Where's this young man of yours?"

The blue eyes widened for a moment, then the chin lifted. "To whom am I speaking?"

"I," said Van de Velde, "am the captain of this ship."

"And *my* name, Captain, is *Elena Bradbury*. I did not survive merely to be — "

"My dear young lady," he interrupted, "allow me to be blunt. If this companion of yours has not returned to that dugout in exactly one minute — sixty seconds from *now* — it'll be cast off without him, and the next stop for *both* of you will be *Ketchikan!*"

"But there *is* no one else. I came alone!"

The captain allowed his disbelief to show. He turned abruptly. *"Mister Edwards! Coxswain!"* The words were pitched to the other end of the compartment. *"Have you let anyone by?"*

From beyond the crowd, the two men confirmed that no one had left. "Then he's here somewhere," muttered Van de Velde to himself, aware at the same moment of a tap on his elbow.

"It is true, Captain," said Doctor Ramirez softly. "She is alone."

Van de Velde went rigid. Somewhere, someone stifled a giggle. He felt his ears grow hot, and his hand began to rise toward his temple, where a blood vessel had begun to pound, painfully. He caught the gesture in time, pretending he was putting his hand in his pocket.

Captain Van de Velde took a long, slow breath.

"Well!" he declared at last. "That settles that!"

The girl relaxed, ever so slightly. "You're going to save my boat, then?"

It was on the tip of his tongue to say *no*. He wanted to take this creature by the collar and shout his refusal into the salt-streaked young face . . . but then he felt the deck begin to quiver underfoot, and knew that the bridge was following orders. Instead, he smiled his captain's-table smile, and offered his arm. "We'll do the best we can, my dear, I promise you. Here, you can lean on me if you like."

She gazed at him a long moment; then a brief, shy smile appeared. "You don't know what that boat means to me," she said. Her voice was husky. "I think you'd better let one of your men do the assisting, though. My hands are a mess. I'd only leave stains on your uniform." Her smile came again, apologetic now, as she balanced on her one good foot, displaying a pair of bloodied palms.

Such people, he recalled, were often carriers of serum hepatitis. Unable to control his revulsion, he drew back.

Instantly, the girl's eyes hooded. Her mouth tightened, and her right hand returned to its place on the dogging latch. "I'd like to oversee the loading of the boat, if I may."

"I'm afraid that's quite impossible."

"How do you mean — impossible?"

"This ship has a schedule to keep."

The eyes grew angry. "There is no need to interfere with your schedule. Just in the time we've been talking, the boat could have been taken aboard. It's only a moment's work."

The captain laughed, but it was not a pleasant laugh. "So now you tell me my business! You would risk the lives of my men getting that hollowed-out log of yours up to the boat deck? Perhaps you didn't hear me. I am the captain of this ship! Do you have any idea what that means?"

"It means you *ought* to have a grasp of seamanship. For God's sake, use your eyes! With the other half of this door open, the boat'd slip right in, outrigger and all! It wouldn't take more than . . . *twenty seconds* from your schedule! And no risk to your men, either. I myself lifted that boat up a bluff twice as high as this . . . when I had two feet."

The captain was enjoying his triumph. "Too late," he said quietly. The words had the lilt of a school yard taunt. "You see, the ship has *way* now." With a slight motion of his head, he compelled her to look back. And down.

Below, the water slid by, accelerating, breaking into long crests of foam even as they looked. The outrigger had begun to dance, moving out from the ship and in again, like a living thing.

"*Cut it loose, Mister Sawyer.*" The captain's voice was like a lash. He turned, and a path opened for him as he walked away.

He heard a cry behind him. And another. Whirling, he saw the girl was gone. He took one step on his own, and then lost control, finding himself propelled forward in the general rush to the opening. His view was blocked, and he roared to his people to make room, bulling his way through to the door. Below, the girl knelt in the bottom of the boat. She was withdrawing something from her shirt. An aluminum can. Green. It had the picture of a lime on it. The can, with the pull tab unopened, went into the pocket of a disreputable orange jacket. The flap of the pocket was secured. Then, methodically, the girl began putting on the jacket.

"Don't be a fool!" he called. *"You'll be pulled under!"*

No answer. Just a momentary upward glance as she fastened the zipper.

"The screw!" bellowed Van de Velde, pointing toward the mountain of foam astern. Then, thinking she might not comprehend: *"The pro-pell-er! You'll be cut to pieces!"*

"That's what *you* think!" The crewman's hat came sailing up to him. Automatically, he caught it. Below, the outrigger bucked and lunged like a captive horse. The girl tugged at the quick-release knot. The line whipped free, and like a leaf tossed from the window of a moving car, the boat spun away, traveling the length of the ship's long white side. Picking up a paddle-shaped section of board, the girl steadied the craft, so that it headed toward the hump of quick water kicked up by the starboard screw. The boat lifted to it, passed over, and went down the other side, drawn inexorably inward, toward the hull of the ship. The outrigger raced from sight around the curve of the stern.

"Jesus Mary!" whispered one of the stewards. The doctor crossed himself, but said nothing. They all waited.

Van de Velde watched the ship's wake. After half a minute, the outrigger came into view once more. The little figure in the orange jacket sat amidships, paddling steadily for the mainland.